DISCUSSIONS

of

SIMONE WEIL

SUNY series,
Simone Weil Studies

Eric O. Springsted, editor

DISCUSSIONS

of

SIMONE WEIL

RUSH RHEES

Edited by

D. Z. PHILLIPS

Assisted by

Mario von der Ruhr

STATE UNIVERSITY OF NEW YORK PRESS

Published by
STATE UNIVERSITY OF NEW YORK PRESS, ALBANY

© 2000 State University of New York

For information, address State University of New York Press,
State University Plaza, Albany, NY 12246

Production, Laurie Searl
Marketing, Patrick Durocher

Library of Congress Cataloging-in-Publication Data

Rhees, Rush.
    Dicussions of Simone Weil / Rush Rhees ; edited by D.Z. Phillips ; assisted by Mario
von der Ruhr.
        p.   cm. — (SUNY series, Simone Weil studies)
    Includes bibliographical references and indexes.
    ISBN 0-7914-4427-9 (alk. paper) — ISBN 0-7914-4428-7 (pbk. : alk. paper)
    1. Weil, Simone, 1909–1943. I. Phillips, D.Z. (Dewi Zephaniah) II. Von der Ruhr,
Mario. III. Title. IV. Series.

B2430.W474 R45 2000
194—dc21   99-045377

10   9   8   7   6   5   4   3   2   1

CONTENTS

EDITOR'S PREFACE

The work of Simone Weil (1909–1943) has not been given the attention it deserves by philosophers in Anglo-American philosophical traditions. There is no longer any excuse for this, given the availability of her work in French and English. Further, discussions of her work which should encourage such interest can be found in Peter Winch's *Simone Weil: "The Just Balance,"* David McLellan's *Simone Weil: Utopian Pessimist,* Richard Bell's edited collection, *Simone Weil's Philosophy of Culture,* and the studies in the Simone Weil series published by SUNY Press. It is to be hoped that the distinctive contribution made by Rush Rhees's discussions will convince new readers that Simone Weil's work repays serious study.

On 1 November 1968, in a letter to Peter Winch, who had just begun teaching a course on Simone Weil, Rhees refers to some of the obstacles which stand in the way of the philosophical appropriation of her work by professional philosophers:

> It is hard to see, or to formulate, what it is one can *learn* from what Simone Weil writes. She is not writing about the questions discussed in the philosophical periodicals. The most superficial view would be that if you can learn from what she says, then she must say something that you yourself will be prepared to assert and adopt. Nobody who is used to philosophy ought to think that way; but I guess some of them do.
>
> Her work is so foreign to the habits of thinking of most people there. I was going to speak of a provincialism, parochialism in our thinking, but these are not the right expressions. The fact that she is French is part of what makes it hard for people to fit her into their pockets. But I would bet that there are many philosophers in France who show the same kind of impatience, the same sort of misunderstanding, the same objection to having to *try* to follow what she says, that people do here.

> If people can be brought to loosen up their joints a bit; if they can be brought to see that there are other questions and other ways of thinking about them, it will have been worth doing. Not that the people will then be inclined to ask such questions or talk about them in these ways themselves; I am not suggesting that. But perhaps they will see that there is something to *try* to understand in what she writes; that this sort of talk cannot just be dismissed as poppy-cock. That would be something. And it might bring them to see the problems differently on which they *are* engaged; it might widen the landscape in which they see these problems. To do this, they will have to *resist* the natural and strong inclination just to dismiss what she says.

In Rhees's own essays we see an engagement with Simone Weil's work by a remarkable thinker. His discussions, however, are not meant to be an introduction to her work. In fact, he was reluctant to discuss Weil with people who were not already thoroughly acquainted with her work, which can be (and is) so easily misrepresented. In M. O'C. Drury, his closest friend, he found someone as seriously interested in Simone Weil as himself. The essays in this collection are, in the main, letters to Drury and notes written between 1962 and 1969. Rhees was one of the earliest readers of Weil once her work became available in France. He wrote for himself with no thought of publication. Despite the high regard for her work that is evident in his discussions, it is the difficulties he encountered which prevail. That must be borne in mind in reading the collection.

Rhees's discussions fall into three broad categories: social philosophy, science and necessity, and reflections on ethics and religion.

In his discussions of Simone Weil's social philosophy, Rhees thinks the development in her thought constitutes an important contribution to the subject. He criticises her early attempts to give a homogeneous account of "the organisation of society" and finds a genuine advance in her later discussions of the soul's need for roots of various kinds.

It is in his discussions of science and necessity, without doubt, that Rhees has greatest difficulty with Weil's work after 1939. Before that date, he finds that he can engage with her philosophy of science in a philosophical style which comes naturally to him. Later he is frequently at a loss to know whether what she writes should be read as philosophy of science or as a form of religious meditation. If he reads her philosophically, obvious objections occur to him. For example, he finds her ignoring distinctions between mathematical, physical, and moral necessity. He does not see how she can say that a chemical reaction or the movement of the tides can be seen as a model of perfect obedience which we should be able to make use of in our own lives. Rhees does not see how this way of talking can show us anything about the love of God, and he regrets that Weil pursued these harmful analogies. On the other hand, in making such criticisms, Rhees says that he often feels he is being stupid, because he knows she is not making a simple blunder. How she views science itself depends on her relation to God, and on an aspect of that relation to which Rhees thinks he may be blind. But Weil spoke in this way to the end, and to the end, also, it created a difficulty for Rhees about how to read her work. For this reason, while Rhees thought she was an extremely important philosopher, he did not think she was a great one. To him, she did not seem to be aware, or at least did not see the need to discuss, obvious differences between science and religion which need to be addressed. Rhees's discussions give us, however, the most sustained critique to date of Weil's views on science and religion.

Rhees thought that Simone Weil's greatness, though *greatness* is probably the wrong word, is to be found in her reflections on ethics and religion. He thought of her as a saint. In her remarks on human affliction, for instance, Rhees found a depth he had not found in others, including St. Paul, Augustine, and Kierkegaard. He had an immense regard for Kierkegaard, but he thought that Weil was the deeper religious thinker. What drew him to her was her intellectual probity in discussing central religious questions: the kind of reality God can be said to have, the difference between suffering and affliction, what loving God means, and the significance of death. Rhees admired the way in which Weil strove for, and often attained, a nakedness of style in which nothing is said with a flourish or for the sake of effect. Rhees was depressed and even disgusted by the way serious moral and religious questions were often discussed in contemporary philosophy. He found, in Simone Weil, a profound and rare exception.

This is connected with the reason why, despite his emphasis on difficulties and disagreements with Weil, Rhees's discussions of her work need to be presented: the same intellectual probity which he so admired in Simone Weil was characteristic of Rhees himself. As a result, there is a great deal to learn from his discussions. Further, Rhees's concentration on difficulties counters the easy tendency for religious admiration of Simone Weil to lead to an uncritical acceptance of everything she says.

It also counters the opposite easy tendency to misrepresent her views from a lack of sympathy for religion. In contrast to both reactions, Simone Weil has, in Rush Rhees, a fellow enquirer who does justice to the depth of her reflections.

Rush Rhees taught at the University College of Swansea from 1940 to 1966. Among his principal teachers Rhees counted John Anderson at Edinburgh, Alfred Kastil at Innsbruck, G. E. Moore and, above all, Ludwig Wittgenstein at Cambridge. After his early retirement, Rhees lived for a period in London and Cambridgeshire. He returned to Swansea late in life where he became an Honorary Professor and Fellow of the College.

After his death in 1989, the Department of Philosophy purchased Rhees's papers. He had turned down requests to work on them, counting them as "nothing." No one else shared his judgement. The papers turned out to be sixteen thousand pages of manuscript, made up of notes and letters on every branch of philosophy. Rhees had published little during his lifetime, devoting much of his energy, in this respect, to making Wittgenstein's work available. Rhees was one of Wittgenstein's literary executors. I had been instrumental in persuading Rhees to publish two collections of essays, *Without Answers* (1969) and *Discussions of Wittgenstein* (1970) published by Routledge and Kegan Paul. The collections show Rhees to be a remarkable philosopher in his own right but give no indication of *how* remarkable. To appreciate that, one needs to appreciate the intellectual breadth and depth of the papers which make up his Archive. This is one reason why I have undertaken, with the help of others, to make more of his work available. The purchase of Rhees's papers was made possible through the A. E. Heath Memorial Fund established through the generosity of Mrs. Heath. A. E. Heath was Foundation Professor of Philosophy at Swansea from 1925 to 1952.

Papers from the Rush Rhees Archive have been published in the journal *Philosophical Investigations*. *Discussions of Simone Weil* is the fifth book to be edited from the Archive. The first, *On Religion and Philosophy* (Cambridge University Press, 1997) is one of the most impressive collections in the philosophy of religion in the twentieth century. The second, *Wittgenstein and the Possibility of Discourse* (Cambridge University Press, 1998) is a far-reaching critique of Wittgenstein's *Philosophical Investigations* in the course of discussing what it means to say something and the unity of discourse. I have provided a biographical sketch of Rhees in the first two volumes. The third, *Wittgenstein's 'On Certainty'*, is Rhees's discussion of Wittgenstein's frequently misunderstood work and related issues. The fourth, *Moral Questions* (Macmillan, 1999), is an attack on moral theory and the claim that moral philosophy can guide our conduct. Rhees also discusses a range of substantive moral issues.

I have provided the dates for Rhees's *Discussions of Simone Weil* so that readers who are so inclined can follow the chronology of his observations. I am responsible for the titles of the papers and of the book. I am also responsible for all the divisions within the texts. The final order which these have taken owed much to a valuable discussion with Richard Bell.

I am indebted to my assistant editor, Mario von der Ruhr, for preparing the biographical and bibliographical sketch of Simone Weil and the list of her publications, for his extensive tracing of bibliographical sources, for his checking of quotations, for matching the French originals and the English translations, and for his preparation of the index of names and subjects. I am also grateful to him and my colleague Timothy Tessin for proofreading the collection, and to Mrs. Helen Baldwin, Secretary to the Department of Philosophy at Swansea, for preparing the typescript for publication from my handwritten text.

PART ONE

SOCIAL PHILOSOPHY

CHAPTER ONE

METHOD AND LIBERTY

In *Oppression and Liberty*[1] Simone Weil says that to be deprived of liberty robs life of its value (see p. 85). Here "liberty" does not mean "being able to do whatever you wish." "True liberty is not defined by a relationship between a desire and its satisfaction, but by a relationship between thought and action" (p. 85). Such a relation is found in certain forms of *manual labour*—for example that of skilled craftsmen. So she will argue (see p. 104) that the freest society would be one in which manual labour was most highly esteemed, and "Man would then have his fate constantly in his own hands" (p. 87). In the same way she describes slavery as a condition in which a man does *not* have his life in his own hands.

If we say this is possible, we should still recognize that what I do, the life I lead, is limited by the special time and place in which I live, by the hardships and misfortunes I meet, by the death of friends and those on whom I depend, by obstacles I could never have foreseen, etc., etc. But the way I try to meet these difficulties, the possibilities I recognize and the decisions I make, the methods I try and (often) the methods I *refuse* to try—or also my capitulation when I give up—these are "my own doing."

Simone Weil's *method* in this section follows in some respects the use of geometry in physics; also the use of theoretical *models* in physics; the notion of 'ideal cases'. She may have been influenced by Descartes's method of analysis into "simple elements." She starts with an "abstract model" of "completely free activity"—the activity of thought in solving a problem in arithmetic. She then considers the limitations and modifications which must be made when we pass from this to solving problems in physics, in engineering; and finally to the activities in which people are engaged with others in a society.

This helps her to bring out some things. Consider, for instance, her picture of a free community, her "purely theoretical" sketch of the conditions that would make the "material life" (i.e., the productive, economic life) of a community free from social oppression.

> Thus, if we wish to form, in a purely theoretical way, the conception of a society in which collective life would be subject to men as individuals instead of subjecting them to itself, we must visualize a form of material existence wherein only efforts exclusively directed by a clear intelligence would take place, which would imply that each worker himself had to control, without referring to any external rule, not only the adaptation of his efforts to the piece of work to be produced, but also their co-ordination with the efforts of all the other members of the collectivity. The technique would have to be such as to make continual use of methodical thought; the analogy between the techniques employed in the various tasks would have to be sufficiently close, and technical education sufficiently widespread, to enable each worker to form a clear idea of all the specialized procedures; co-ordination would have to be arranged in sufficiently simple a manner to enable one continually to have a precise knowledge of it, as concerns both co-operation between workers and exchange of products; collectivities would never be sufficiently vast to pass outside the range of a human mind; community of interests would be sufficiently patent to abolish competitive attitudes; and as each individual would be in a position to exercise control over the collective life as a whole, the latter would always be in accordance with the general will. Privileges founded upon the exchange of products, secrets of production or the co-ordination of labour would automatically be done away with. The function of co-ordinating would no longer imply power, since a continual check exercised by each individual would render any arbitrary decision impossible. Generally speaking, men's dependence with regard to one another would no longer imply that their fate rested in the hands of arbitrary factors, and would cease to introduce into human life any mysterious element whatever, since each would be in a position to verify all the activities of all the rest by using his own reason. There is but one single and identical reason for all men; they only become estranged from and impenetrable to each other when they depart from it; thus

a society in which the whole of material existence had as its necessary and sufficient condition that each individual should exercise his
reason could be absolutely clearly understood by each individual
mind. As for the stimulus necessary to overcome fatigue, sufferings,
and dangers, each would find it in the desire to win the esteem of his
fellows, but even more so in himself; in the case of creative work by
the mind, outward constraint, having become useless and harmful, is
replaced by a sort of inward constraint; the sight of the unfinished
task attracts the free man as powerfully as the overseer's whip stim-
ulates the slave. Such a society alone would be a society of men free,
equal and brothers. Men would, it is true, be bound by collective ties,
but exclusively in their capacity as men; they would never be treated
by each other as things. Each would see in every work-fellow
another self occupying another past, and would love him in the way
that the Gospel maxim enjoins. Thus we should possess, over and
above liberty, a still more precious good; for if nothing is more odi-
ous than the humiliation and degradation of man by man, nothing is
so beautiful or so sweet as friendship.[2] (pp. 98–100)

She does not suggest that what she sketches could ever exist. The
sketch is to give a standard by which to measure the liberality or oppressiveness of communities that do exist or may exist.

"The above picture considered by itself, is, if possible, still farther
removed from the actual conditions of human existence than is the fiction of a Golden Age. But, unlike that fiction, it is able to serve, by way
of an ideal, as a standard for the analysis and evaluations of actual social
patterns" (p. 100).[3]

But is it satisfactory as a standard? We are deprived of liberty and
we know only that this robs life of its value (see p. 85). We want to make
our aspirations clearer—to become clear about the liberty we want.
Does Simone Weil's sketch in this place look like an answer?

It would seem as though Simone Weil had been blinded by the
abstract model which she thought she must construct if she was to follow precise methods at all. And something of the same applies to her
conception of 'thinking' and her use of this to distinguish free activities
from servile ones. She writes as though we could speak of "social organization" apart from the histories and other features of societies. And
similarly, she writes as though "thinking" were one activity or process—
perhaps comparable to "respiration"—which we could recognize anywhere, and which would be the same process wherever it might be.

But it would be confusing and mistaken, I think, to suggest that we always mean the same—in the sense of "the same activity"—whenever we speak of thinking. Was there no thinking before there was method (i.e., what *we* should recognize as method)? This may show the value of Marx's pronouncement that "social existence determines consciousness," although he made confused use of this.

One reason for taking *thinking* as a paradigm of free activity is that thinking cannot be brought about by force—a man cannot be forced to think. Although in a sense he can. And "forced to think" is a common expression. But she means "not by commands, threats and penalties." She distinguishes here between *thinking* in the sense of calculating, investigating, testing, criticizing,—and *imagination* which may go with terror or unfulfilled desire. It might have made her essay clearer if she had been more explicit and more detailed on this.

But this does not show much about the control of action by thought. It almost looks as though she was suggesting that *method* enables me to control my life just as it enables me or men to control natural forces perhaps when I build a dam or a bridge. "Thinking is making plans." Does a man who *plans* his actions, his life, *control* the course of his life to a greater extent than the man who does not plan? For example, a methodical businessman more than an artist? An artist who, perhaps, brings little method to the conduct of his life, although he may keep to certain standards—rejecting what would be a betrayal of his art (but without making plans).

Do I by making plans control the course of my life, whether my plans do generally fail or generally succeed? "When your plans have failed you can *learn* from this: you can investigate to find out where your mistake was. If you made no plans, you cannot learn—or not in this way." But learning where my mistake was does not always enable me to "correct it" in the sense of avoiding that sort of pitfall in the future. "I make up these sex rules for myself, and then. . . ." Here the analogy with solving mathematical or theoretical problems does not serve.

The danger that someone devoted to 'method' will be inflexible and have very restricted vision. Simone Weil speaks later in the essay of a servility to computers and generally to instruments. May there not be a comparable servility to "methodical procedures" and especially to analogies with problems in mathematics and in technology? Obviously there are certain activities in which planning is important (or indispensable) as it is not in others. A mariner must plot his course, check his position, distance travelled, and so on.

The reason why she concentrates on 'thinking' in her special sense—with the paradigm in doing mathematics—seems to be this: she is thinking of mathematical or logical rules, rules of thinking, as contrasted with natural laws. "Events in nature do not proceed from the clearer and the simpler to the more complex and difficult." *Internal* relations in logic, as contrasted with *external* relations which are discovered by experiment. It is as though she were unable to give an account of the distinction between thinking—"what is *peculiar* or *proper* to thinking"—and material events in any other way. "In thinking the sequence is guided by intelligence, in material processes it is not."

Even with certain occupations—a navigator for instance—where planning is particularly necessary, it does not follow that a navigator is more in control of the course of his life than is an artist who lives without making plans, or than a mendicant pilgrim is. "But surely the mendicant pilgrim is dependent constantly on the wills—the charity—of others?" "To the extent to which a man's fate is dependent on other men, his own life escapes not only out of his hands, but also out of the control of his intelligence; judgement and resolution no longer have anything to which to apply themselves; instead of contriving and acting, one has to stoop to pleading or threatening; and the soul is plunged into bottomless abysses of desire and fear, for there are no bounds to the satisfactions and sufferings that a man can receive at the hands of other men" (p. 96).[4] Yes. But this raises the question of what "controlling *the course* of his life" is. For suppose it was by his own decision (his own will) that he came to lead this sort of mendicant life.

The notion of 'self-discipline'—does this come in here? "Character is self-discipline." The difference between self-discipline and military discipline. Granting that self-discipline is needed in a soldier, this is something different.

Simone Weil's comparison with working on a poem or painting. Notice that this comparison leads away from distinctions of means and ends in connexion with the life one is trying to lead. We might say that self-discipline *is* controlling one's life.

His own action: what comes from *him*. We may speak of 'originality' in this sense: without meaning that he is "doing something new." (I'll show my originality by having my own arithmetic; first in the field; the man who discovered, gave his name to . . .)

"Mut ist immer originell." (Courage is always original.)

Simone Weil writes: "A clear view of what is possible and what impossible, what is easy and what difficult, of the labours that separate the project from its accomplishment—this alone does away with insatiable desires and vain fears; from this and not from anything else proceed moderation and courage, virtues without which life is nothing but a disgraceful frenzy."[5]

It is interesting and important that she does bring these in here: that she thinks courage (and purity) are somehow fundamental to liberty— no less so, I imagine, than are the features of solving arithmetical problems which she has mentioned.

She claims that these virtues grow *only* from "a clear view of what is possible and impossible." In what sense? Often courage is demanded and shown where the man does *not* have a clear view of what is possible and impossible—in regard to external circumstances and also in regard to what he can expect of himself. If "impossible" means *unthinkable*—as we might say, *morally* unthinkable: "What are you asking me to do? Are you *crazy*?"—this is different. But in that passage she is not speaking of this.

Simone Weil may be exploring a comparison between "the values of science" and "the values of art." The notion of 'the pursuit of truth for its own sake' was a protest against certain forms of instrumentalism and pragmatism which were themselves a revolt against it. See Marxist views of science, benevolence, raising the lot of man, the domination of science by engineering, the treatment of mathematics as a game, an obsession with problems because they are puzzling, the satisfaction of reaching a solution, "an achievement," fields in which one may gain prestige.

Contrast with this "Helping men to understand their relation to the world," "removal of superstition," explanation of what had seemed inexplicable, enlightenment versus obscurantism, knowing what you are faced with—not a slave to your own fears and imagination.

There is also something important—or may be—in the notion of 'being scientific,' for example, *toward* some problems and difficulties. It becomes stupid when the difficulty is one to which this "investigation to discover what the facts are, measurement, etc." is not applicable. Even 'being methodical' may, in certain problems—for certain decisions—be stupid, may be a form of evasion.

Simone Weil emphasizes the connexion of science (which she seems sometimes to regard as what is meant by *pensée*) with application, in order to make clear the notion of living a life of freedom, as opposed to slavery. Responsibility: deciding what course to take in view of one's own understanding of the situation in which one is placed.

There is still room for considerable ambiguity here. Perhaps especially in the analogy between scientific or engineering problems and the problem of what is the best course to take. "The scientific answer."

In *Oppression and Liberty* Weil is trying to explain the hold which a way of thinking had on Marx and his followers; and the way in which it prevented them from criticism or examination of their conception of 'revolution'. What she brings out is the trust which Marx had in science, and the idea that the growth of science (which he often read as the growth of technology) would *liberate* man (whatever that may have meant). So that men could lead their *own* lives rather than submit to a form of life that was imposed on them.

She says: "All religions make men into a mere instrument of Providence, and socialism, too" (p. 45).[6] This leaves out the contrast she would have drawn later between *necessity* and *grace*. She would have said (in most respects, apparently) "l'homme est un simple instrument de la nécessité—ou de la *force*," as the warriors of the *Iliad* were "instruments" of the war in which they were engaged. She says that "we find in Marx a different conception . . . namely, a materialism which no longer has anything religious about it and forms not a doctrine but a method of understanding and of action" (p. 45).[7]

It seems to me a deep misunderstanding to speak of any sort of scientific method for removing injustice (especially if this means "injustice in general"—not this specific injustice which is being committed now). It suggests that we might identify justice—or perhaps liberty—by the way in which it was brought about. It seems to emphasize an analogy with health or disease.

One way in which this is misleading is in her close association of *oppression* with *force*, which she wants to take in the sense of 'force' in physics. This is partly because she wants to emphasize the way in which men are caught up in developments, such as war, for instance, or the struggle for political power in which they seem to be *driven* and more often than not victims. Cf. Lenin's "vehicles of social forces."

The difficulty is that she speaks as though it should be possible to *formulate laws* and *assign causes*, although she does not really suggest any.

When she spoke later of "a science of the supernatural" (or "a science of supernatural intervention") which should be no less rigorous and precise than physics, this was probably in the wish to find a method of distinguishing *idolatry*, or a test of idolatry. Feeling rightly that confusions in one's thinking on these matters are, if anything, more objectionable than confusions in accounts of natural happenings.

But granting the need for clarity and criticism here, one first matter should be to see the difference between the clarity sought here and the clarity sought in physics. A *theory* of the supernatural, in the sense of a scientific theory which may be tested by experiment, cannot be what she wanted.

A method for producing a society (or for changing a given society into one) in which individual men will act with justice towards one another—or act with compassion or charity towards one another—seems as confused an idea as a method for producing a society of high culture (for example in arts and sciences).

One can say "the popular view of tuberculosis is wrong, for tuberculosis has such and such features"; or "the popular view of 'hereditary disease' is wrong or mistaken, for a disease is hereditary. . . ." But not in this way: "the popular view of liberty or of injustice is wrong," as though here also the 'view' were a view, or theory, regarding what happens.

Marx could say that commonly accepted views on the nature of capitalist profits were wrong (for example, regarding "what they come from")—in a sense analogous to that in which we speak of hereditary disease. It is true that some attempts to remedy injustice may be more stupid and others less so. But this is not comparable, for example, to more stupid and less stupid treatment of a disease: for being the less stupid course is that which (inter alia) knows something about the infection, say, and especially knows something of previous experiences and experiments of others in connexion with it. "The previous experience and treatment of injustice" seems irrelevant and meaningless. You cannot legislate for the removal of injustice, still less so for the promotion of justice. You cannot legislate for liberty. "It must come from *him*." It cannot be a subject of *planning*.

"The subjective factor." The need to take account of spontaneous independent activities in any political society, of initiatives which do not come from the government. Legalistic treatments (such as the contract theorists) hardly provide this.

This is connected with Simone Weil's taking solving a mathematical problem as the paradigm of free—not servile—activity. "Because here you are not simply carrying out instructions: you have a reason for each move you make, that is, you know why it must be done and that it is not simply that so and so has ordered it. You make your own decisions and carry them out." The idea of "acting intelligently," or being guided by your understanding in what you do. "So that what I do depends on me (I am responsible)."

But this could be said of art as well as of mathematics. Weil would have agreed, at least in her later work. And this could be said of friendship and generosity. If you cannot force anyone to think, you cannot force him to be generous either. Nor to give artistic criticism.

If someone solves a mathematical problem, he is using expressions he has learned and he is employing methods he has learned. Further: there would not be what we call 'mathematics' nor 'mathematical problems' unless there were a difference between 'correct' and 'incorrect', unless there were an established practice of mathematics. I may find the solution on my own, but I do not invent mathematics on my own—that means nothing.

There are different cases of following a rule. "Following a rule I can understand," "Now I see how it goes," "now I can go on," "now I can find the solution myself." What is the difference when I am "following a rule—command, order—which I do not understand"—or blindly carrying out instructions? Do I understand the rules printed on the box of the game I buy in Woolworth's? We should hardly call this "blind obedience," "blindly carrying out instructions," nor say that it is sensible of me to follow them. Partly because of this notion of "understanding the game," knowing how to play according to the rules, and, in this sense, understanding them, I know "what to do" in such and such a situation in the game.

A bank clerk may unlock the door of the bank when a man holds a gun to his head and tells him to unlock it. (Or because of blackmail, etc.) This is something he would not do were it not for the threat. (But could I say that what he does "depends on *him*"?)

"Receiving the order," "being told the rule" (of mathematics or a game). "Do you understand what he is telling you to do?" "Do you understand the rule?" The sign, expression, or assurance that I do understand the rule is: "Now I can go on by myself." There is nothing of this sort when I understand what the man with the gun is telling me to do.

Simone Weil seems to suggest that it is similar when a factory worker is told the moves to make in operating a machine. (Or is this *not* what she means?) Cf. "A man would be completely a slave if all his movements proceeded from a source other than his mind, namely, either the irrational reactions of the body, or else the mind of other people; primitive man, ravenous, his every bound provoked by the spasms tearing at his belly, the Roman slave perpetually keyed up to execute the orders of an overseer with a whip, the manual worker of our own day engaged in a production line, all these approach the wretched condition" (p. 86).[8]

She speaks of complete liberty (la liberté complète) (p. 86). I do not think this means anything except when it is *contrasted* with some form of oppression or some form of servitude. And I do not know what the servitude would be which is contrasted with solving the problem in arithmetic. Is *this* "which takes away the value from life" (p. 85)?[9] This has something to do with her method of investigation, her use of an abstract model here. (Why am I not "complètement libre" when I am playing table tennis?)

She writes: "a completely free life would be one wherein all real difficulties presented themselves as kinds of problems, wherein all successes were as solutions carried into action" (p. 86).[10] I wonder how she would work this out; how she would illustrate "presented themselves as."

Again: "Man would then have his fate constantly in his own hands; at each moment he would forge the conditions of his own existence by an act of mind."[11] This is important: in the same way she describes slavery as the condition in which a man does *not* have "son propre sort—on sa propre vie—en mains." But the model is still very abstract, as appears when you try to imagine an actual case.

Is Simone Weil's method—starting with an "ideal" or "perfect" case, examining the deviations in actual practice, asking what causes these, and so on—is this an appropriate method for analysis of 'liberty' or 'oppression'? Trying to give an account of the relation of thought and action, and in this sense of having one's life in one's own hands, not being the plaything of blind forces, and such.

I do not think she does follow this method in *The Need for Roots* (*L'Enracinement*). And this is connected with the importance she attaches there to *collectivité* and *le passée*. The "needs of the soul" go far beyond "the fate which is in his own hands" (son propre sort en mains). And her different attitude towards "legitimate government" goes with this.

The intolerable character who calculates the possible chances before any and every action. (Insurance to cover risks. A *commercial* view.) "It is worth doing whether it seems foolhardy or not." If we were always engaged in engineering, the case would be different.

"Trying to decide what to do—trying to decide how to live." In the second on "une société libre" she is asking how far or in what way free action or a free life is conceivable—in any society. There is point in starting as she does with the action or life of an *individual*, but this need not have led to the degree of abstraction she keeps. This, as we shall see, is reflected in the way in which she speaks of "*the* organization of society."

NOTES

From Notes dated 26.2.68; 28.2.68; 11.3.68; 12.3.68.

1. *Oppression and Liberty*, trans. Arthur Wills and John Petrie, Amherst: University of Massachusetts Press, 1973. All quotations from this edition. French edition: *Oppression et Liberté*, Paris: Gallimard, 1955.

2. "Ainsi, si l'on veut former, d'une manière purement théorique, la conception d'une société où la vie collective serait soumise aux hommes considérés en tant qu'individus au lieu de se les soumettre, il faut se représenter une forme de vie matérielle dans laquelle n'interviendraient que des efforts exclusivement dirigés par la pensée claire, ce qui impliquerait que chaque travailleur ait lui-même à contrôler, sans se référer à aucune règle extérieure, non seulement l'adaptation de ses efforts avec l'ouvrage à produire, mais encore leur coordination avec les efforts de tous les autres membres de la collectivité. La technique devrait être de nature à mettre perpétuellement à l'oeuvre la réflexion méthodique; l'analogie entre les techniques des différents travaux devrait être assez étroite et la culture technique assez étendue pour que chaque travailleur se fasse une idée nette de toutes les spécialités; la coordination devrait s'établir d'une manière assez simple pour que chacun en ait perpétuellement une connaissance précise, en ce qui concerne la coopération des travailleurs aussi bien que les échanges des produits; les collectivités ne seraient jamais assez étendues pour dépasser la portée d'un esprit humain; la communauté des intérêts serait assez évidente pour effacer les rivalités; et comme chaque individu serait en état de contrôler l'ensemble de la vie collective, celle-ci serait toujours conforme à la volonté générale. Les privilèges fondés sur l'échange des produits, les secrets de la production ou la coordination des travaux se trouveraient automatiquement abolis. La fonction de coordonner n'impliquerait plus aucune puissance, puisqu'un contrôle continuel exercé par chacun rendrait toute décision arbitraire impossible. D'une manière générale la dépendance des hommes les uns vis-à-vis des autres n'impliquerait plus que leur sort se trouve livré à l'arbitraire, et elle cesserait d'introduire dans la vie humaine quoi que ce soit de mystérieux, puisque chacun serait en état de contrôler l'activité de tous les autres en faisant appel à sa seule raison. Il n'y a qu'une seule et même raison pour tous les

hommes; ils ne deviennent étrangers et impénétrables les uns aux autres que lors-qu'ils s'en écartent; ainsi une société où toute la vie matérielle aurait pur condi-tion nécessaire et suffisante que chacun exerce sa raison pourrait être tout à fait transparente pour chaque esprit. Quant au stimulant nécessaire pour surmonter les fatigues, les douleurs et les dangers, chacun le trouverait dans le désir d'obtenir l'estime de ses compagnons, mais plus encore en lui-même; pour les travaux qui sont des créations de l'esprit, la contrainte extérieure, devenue inutile et nuisible, est remplacée par une sorte de contrainte intérieure; le spec-tacle de l'ouvrage inachevé attire l'homme libre aussi puissamment que le fouet pousse l'esclave. Une telle société serait seule une société d'hommes libres, égaux et frères. Les hommes seraient à vrai dire pris dans des liens collectifs, mais exclusivement en leur qualité d'hommes; ils ne seraient jamais traités les uns par les autres comme des choses. Chacun verrait en chaque compagnon de travail un autre soi-même placé à un autre poste, et l'aimerait comme le veut la maxime évangélique. Ainsi l'on posséderait en plus de la liberté un bien plus précieux encore; car si rien n'est plus odieux que l'humiliation et l'avilissement de l'homme par l'homme, rien n'est si beau ni si doux que l'amitié." Simone Weil, *Oppression et Liberté*, Paris: Gallimard, 1955, pp. 130–32.

3. "Ce tableau, considéré en lui-même, est si possible plus éloigné encore des conditions réelles de la vie humaine que la fiction de l'âge d'or. Mais à la différence de cette fiction il peut servir, en tant qu'idéal, de point de repère pur l'analyse et l'ap-préciation des formes sociales réelles." *Oppression et Liberté*, p. 132.

4. "Dans la mesure où le sort d'un homme dépend d'autres hommes, sa propre vie échappe non seulement à ses mains, mais aussi à son intelligence; le jugement et la résolution n'ont plus rien à quoi s'appliquer; au lieu de combiner et d'agir, il faut s'abaisser à supplier ou à menacer; et l'âme tombe dans des gouf-fres sans fond de désir et de crainte, car il n'y a pas de limites aux satisfactions et aux souffrances qu'un homme peut recevoir des autres hommes." *Oppression et Liberté*, pp. 127–28.

5. "Une vue claire du possible et de l'impossible, du facile et du difficile, des paines qui séparent le projet de l'accomplissements efface seule les désirs insatiables et les craintes vaines; de là et non d'ailleurs procèdent la tempérance et le courage, vertus sans lesquelles la vie n'est qu'un honteux délire." Simone Weil, *Oppression et Liberté*, Paris: Gallimard, 1955, p. 117.

6. "Toutes les religions font de l'homme un simple instrument de la Prov-idence, et le socialisme lui aussi." *Oppression et Liberté*, p. 66.

7. "On trouve chez Marx une autre conception . . . à savoir un matérial-isme qui n'a plus rien de religieux et constitue non pas une doctrine, mais une méthode de connaissance et d'action." Ibid., p. 67.

8. "Un homme serait complètement esclave si tous ces gestes procédaient d'une autre source que sa pensée, à savoir ou bien les réactions irraisonnées du

corps, ou bien la pensée d'autrui; l'homme primitif affamé dans tous les bonds sont provoqués par les spasmes qui tordent ses entrailles, l'esclave romain perpétuellement tendu vers les ordres d'un surveillant armé d'un fouet, l'ouvrier moderne qui travaille à la chaîne, approchent de cette condition misérable." *Oppression et Liberté*, p. 116.

    9. "ce dont la privation ôte à la vie sa valeur." *Oppression et Liberté*, p. 115.

    10. "Une vie entièrement libre serait celle où toutes les difficultés réelles se présenteraient comme des sortes de problèmes, où toutes les victoires seraient comme des solutions mises en action." Ibid., p. 116.

    11. "L'homme aurait alors constamment son propre sort en mains; il forgerait à chaque moment les conditions de sa propre existence par un acte de la pensée." Ibid., pp. 116–17.

CHAPTER TWO

"*The* Organization of Society"

In *Oppression and Liberty* Simone Weil discusses the notion of an oppressive *regime*, rather than the ruthlessness of particular individuals or groups in positions of power. And this is important.

It is the way things are done (we may almost want to say "the way things *happen*," but this is wrong)—the way production and exchange are carried on when there is large-scale industry—it is this which reduces workers to servitude. (In fact: reduces *all* men living under this regime to servitude.)

Simone Weil speaks of "the social organization" (or "the organization of society"). But why "*the* organization"? Marxists speak in a similar way of "the *structure* of a society"; they say this depends on the conditions of production, for instance. Of course Marx and Simone Weil would say there have been societies of different structures, or different organization at different historical periods; in medieval Europe the organization of society was not what it was in nineteenth-century Europe, for instance. But consider the society of Great Britain in 1968 and ask, "What is the organization (or the structure) of this society at the present time?" Is only one answer possible?

Marx and Weil assume it must be *economic* organization, organization for production. And they do not even consider other ways in which the society might be described. Perhaps in terms of literacy, of the readership of existing newspapers, or the devotion to various radio programmes, of town living and country living, and so on.

If one speaks of "*the* organization" of our society, this may go with some idea of an end or purpose of the society; something which the operation of the society (like the operation of a factory) should produce. Some complex *work* of production on which we are all engaged. We see some signs and consequences of this assumption when Simone Weil describes a theoretical model of a free society.

It is easier to notice this confusion than it is to keep from falling into it. Marx and Weil were trying to get us to look at society in a different way. Or, in Weil's case, to look at the relations between society and individuals in a different way. If one tries to do this, one will almost certainly direct attention to "this aspect." Rather as if you were trying to get me to see something important about a particular cathedral, and you tried to get me to look at everything in relation to this door or this tower. "Get hold of *this*, and then you'll see."

For Simone Weil the point is that certain forms of social organization are more oppressive, and others less so. But in this essay she gives too little attention to organizations that oppose or resist one another. For example, *within* industry there are organizations of trades unions, as opposed to business (commercial) organizations of factory management and such. She emphasizes that even within trade unions—as also in working-class political parties—the separation of "direction" and "performance" (those who decide policy and those who do the donkey work) appears again. This is true. But the workers are not subject only to *one* overriding organization. And since there are opposing organizations, workers have some chance for initiative, some chance of influencing what course is taken.

Political oppression is never *simply* political. The force with which a government rules, the force it exercises, is "the force of the society." Marx saw this. On the other hand, both he and Simone Weil neglected the character of political power and were wont to speak as though all power were the same and all oppression were the same (whether it be political, military, economic, ecclesiastical, or some other). The character of political power can never be wholly independent of these others. But it is not related to them as a civil service ("bureaucratic machine") is related to a government. Political power is not the power to accomplish some special result. To say that political power "is only a means" (p. 69) would be just a mistake. A means to *what*? Simone Weil recognizes this, though confusedly, when she says that in this case the means is treated as an end. But this does nothing to explain the kind of power it is.

Political power is not the same as the power which comes with certain privileges: for example, the power of the expert, the power of the manager of a large bank, and so on. Because she leaves this unclear, she does not bring out the character of *political* oppression in this essay. In her later work she does so.[1]

On the other hand, to speak of *purely* political oppression would—in most cases—be less satisfactory still. Further, we should hardly expect to find a wholly oppressive regime with a markedly liberal government; "it sounds nonsensical." There is some connexion between the ruling policies of a state and the character of life in the society. This leaves it vague. But it would need discussion in any account of political oppression. ("The *government's* not oppressive; it is only doing what . . .")

Simone Weil seems to say: if there is not to be social oppression, then all the people in the community must be taking part in some common enterprise, rather like workers in one workshop or factory trying to produce one product to which all contribute, or perhaps a shipyard in which just one ship is being built, or perhaps the crew of a fishing or cargo ship at sea. Or if she does not think of some common enterprise in this way, then at any rate she imagines people engaged in forms of work which are closely enough related so that each could understand the technique that was being used by each and all of the others.

There would be nothing one could call "the *society's* affairs" that would be separate from the various affairs of individual citizens. In a free (or human) society there must be nothing *mysterious*. There must be nothing in the activities of any man which cannot be understood by every other man. This prevents the growth of experts as a privileged minority, whose word we must accept without understanding it.

But this is a misconceived and "external" view of "living together" and of society. No man, or no particular groups, could engage in any serious undertakings at all. It seems like saying (although Simone Weil would not have said this): "The only significance of any activity is its *economic* significance; and *everyone* can discuss this." It ignores the important distinction between private affairs and public affairs. Without his personal interests, affairs, worries, a man would bring nothing to his work. They make him the man he is, at least as much as his job does.

Simone Weil would answer: she has deliberately given a sketch of the material or economic life, the usual source of social oppression. She does not *deny* personal or other interests. But can an account which is just of the economic or productive relations of human beings help to answer any questions except the questions asked by economists? Can such an account help us to see more clearly what the liberty or oppression of a regime would be?

Marx and Weil in this essay have been led into "blind" abstraction in discussing human societies, for all that Marxists say about "concrete historical."

There is, we may say, a culture in which Italians live, another culture of the Poles, another culture of the Finns. In each case there are characteristic practices and customs, some of them more deep-going than others: the way they carry on agriculture here, the way they build their houses, and so on; these belong to and often illustrate a common heritage, a common history—and with this certain common aspirations—of the people who live in this place. And much of this centres about the *language*. Polish culture will still exist, in some measure, as long as there are Polish newspapers and a Polish theatre. In each case, the culture is connected with a particular territory, and this is not merely an external connexion (as if it might be just the same in another place).

Marx and Marxists have written as though to understand such a society we need only seek to determine the stage of its economic development, whether in this sense the society is "backward" or not. The Italian working class may differ from the Polish working class by being less backward; nothing else makes any difference.

Simone Weil does not use this criterion. She shows the weakness and confusion in the whole idea of "stages" in historical development. But her theoretical sketch of a free society is meant to serve as a standard for measuring the liberality or oppressiveness of *any* society. And here, in this sketch, the relations of production are what count. Science, arts, the personal relations of people to one another are all determined by the "intelligible" relations of production she sketches there. It is as though the existence of a specifically Italian newspaper, an Italian theatre, and so on, in this place makes no difference.

It is important to emphasize that the difference between 'population' and 'society' is not all due to government. But it is not all due to organization or production either. To say this would be to make the same kind of error.

Here it is easy to fall into still worse confusions and mistakes on the other side. The German National Socialists (Hitler) showed this in their propaganda about "blood and soil" (and 'blood', for them, meant 'history' as well). But this propaganda caught on partly because the Marxist doctrine *was* weak and inadequate on this point. The National

Socialists threw in pseudoscience and pseudohistory and used them in support of a *nationalism*—State and Army—which was just as distinctive and disregarding of culture as the most doctrinaire Marxist party could be, or more so. Nationalism in anything like this form comes with a decline of local culture. And it looks very much alike in Italy, Germany, Poland, or where it may be.[2]

There is a sense of "oppression" in which it is degrading, humiliating, as poverty need not be, and as physical disability or physical suffering need not be. Compare Marx's references to what is "dehumanizing," to social conditions or conditions of labour which are "inhuman." There are connections between 'liberty' and 'legal responsibility'. The connexion, perhaps between the notion of legal responsibility and that of 'self-determination'. Responsibility as a citizen. But also "responsibilities towards other citizens" (Social Contract).

One difficulty with this: it suggests that I have not the same responsibilities towards men who are not citizens, that is, men with whom I cannot conclude a *contract*. To discuss an oppressive regime, not in its bearing on the whole population, but only in its relation to citizens—this would be false on various counts. For example, if there are numbers of people who are not citizens, this may be reason for calling the regime oppressive. Some people are *subject* to the regime, although they are not legal subjects or 'persons' in this sense.

People who are in poverty and without employment may be unable to "enter into contractual relations" with those engaged in production, although they are not under any legal disability. In any case, the conditions which permit "freedom of contract" are not easy to determine. Compare discussions of collective bargaining, trade unionism in the nineteenth century, and also more recent discussions of "direction of labour." More recently still, direction of pupils in the studies they shall follow.

The idea of the control of one's life, so that "the course of one's life lies in one's own hands." In what circumstances is this conceivable? Note that Simone Weil inquires into "les *causes* de la liberté et de l'oppression." Suppose one asked rather, "In what does oppression consist?" Or, "What *constitutes* oppression?" To what extent would the discussion be on different lines than in her discussion of "the causes of . . ."? 'Cause' may not always have the same connotation in French and in English. But she seems to use it here as in science.

She is wanting to emphasize that oppression is not the result of human wishes, that is, it cannot be explained by the native disposition towards tyranny in this or that individual, but that it results from "objective conditions" *regardless* of human wishes (materialist view of history). Hence the analogy with "investigation into causes," asking *why* things happen (under what conditions), not whether it is desirable that they should.

Because governments are oppressive, and also because (in states) they are associated with ("the sources of") law and with justice in this sense (crime and punishment), because they become associated with "defense of the country," and with national glory, we are wont to discuss governments in terms of good and evil. This raises the question of "the ideally best polity." Social contract once again. Trying to find some *objective* measures for judgements of value regarding governments.

When people think of "a scientific study of society," the first reaction is commonly to think of a society as a kind of *mechanism*.

It is easy to see that we cannot explain social institutions (an *extremely* vague phrase) or social developments by a psychological study of individuals, or by "human nature" in this sense. On the other hand, we have to turn our attention in the direction of "human psychology"; we have to take account of the difference between human beings and animals, between human *intercourse* and relations between other animals, including the influence of (reflexions on) past history and expectations or plans for the future, if we are to see what sorts of *problems* we are considering: what is meant by a social problem, and what is meant by the *solution* of a social problem.

NOTES

From Notes dated 12.3.68 and 29.4.68.

1. See the section on "Uprootedness and the Nation" in *The Need for Roots*.

2. Cf. *The Need for Roots*, p. 114: "The State eats away (the) moral substance" (of the country).

CHAPTER THREE

LIBERTY AND UNDERSTANDING

Simone Weil's conception of liberty as the measure to which 'la pensée' (meaning, inter alia, initiative) determines one's actions: the geometrical idea of free activity in the solution of a problem in mathematics. Since here the relevant data are all *given*, the solution—or failure to reach a solution—depends on one's own understanding, and not on any external (or not-understood) factors.

Loss of liberty, especially when one has to act from *blind* fear—one is reduced to threats or supplications—of forces one does not understand. (This means in part that one cannot *foresee* the ways in which these forces will operate, cannot see what their limits may be, and cannot meet them or manage them through the intelligent use of instruments.)

She is obviously right in saying that it is not *natural* or material obstacles which are humiliating, or which bring servitude: this can come only from subjection to other human beings. (Although in fact she does not think chiefly of subjection to this or that *individual*. Or perhaps we should say that the subjection to an individual—the slave's subjection to this particular master—shows the operation of a certain *institution*. In this sense it is the "force of the collective" by which the slave is crushed.)

But she does emphasize also that the operator's subjection to the machine—his having to shape his movements, actions, according to the needs of the machine rather than vice versa, a machine which he did not design and perhaps does not understand—is degrading and oppressive (see *Oppression and Liberty*, p. 128 infra). This is a case of *executing* an operation which the worker has not thought out and of which he cannot see the reason. "The separation of intellectual and manual labour."

It is not a question of the laws which have been passed in a society, but of "the conditions of existence," the conditions under which it is possible for individuals to gain a living. The emphasis on the lot of individuals in a way in which the law cannot consider the lot of individuals.

But her explanation of why it is humiliating (degrading, oppressive) for one human being to be at the mercy of another—where it is not degrading or humiliating for a human being to be at the mercy of natural disasters (shipwreck at sea)—is that the *will* of the man to whom I am subject, at whose mercy I am, is not something which can be understood; it is not accessible to *method* or to la pensée, the person subjected cannot foresee (estimate) what will happen, nor see its limits.

This seems like saying, "One is humiliated here because one *cannot* react through the exercise of thinking, and so one is left at the mercy of one's own fears." And this seems to be a logical 'cannot'. But supposing that *in fact* I cannot understand a natural catastrophe—say an earthquake—so far as this affects me at the moment, I cannot be guided in my reaction by my understanding here either. Why should this not be degrading?

But there is a difference. Even if I can see no escape from the earthquake, I do have some idea of what the dangers are. And I do not react by supplications, by *entreating* it. In this sense I am not driven to something degrading; I do not debase myself. It may destroy me, but it does not destroy my self-respect. This is the main point.

But when I *am* driven to abase myself by futile supplications without even giving *reasons* for my supplications—without the dignity of *stating a case* (and this is the difference between a slave and a citizen)—is it really or chiefly because I cannot *understand* the will of him whom I entreat? Suppose I could, and still found myself at his mercy. Would this be comparable to being helpless in an earthquake?

The loss of liberty as something that is humiliating, that makes it impossible to maintain one's self-respect (corrupting in this sense: soul destroying). Making it impossible for me to recover in a sense in which physical suffering need not do this (although, as Simone Weil emphasized later, it often may). The loss of liberty and loss of any opportunity to *labour* with understanding.

Compare Marx. It is not so much a question whether the state is itself the servant of industrialists (or rather, of the capitalist *class*), for Marx does not mean primarily that the government takes *ideas* from any group of industrialists, but rather that its "consciousness" is the consciousness of the capitalist class. The question is rather (is still) whether the state does not reinforce and maintain a certain form of industry: large scale manufacture, centralization, and so on, wherein the worker carries out the "thoughts" of the machine he operates. If this is so, then the state may be *oppressive*, even though it is not (in the normal sense) *tyrannical*.

Simone Weil wants to emphasize that oppression does not depend on the wills of those who exercise it. She wants to study "the objective conditions" in which it is brought about and which prevents its vanishing. She seems to think that this amounts to saying, "it is an operation of natural forces." Probably the vague use of 'la nature' is one source of trouble here. Also, her way of speaking suggests that *force* is the name of a general *sort* of force, or some thing with a way of operating. Compare her remarks on entropy and time.

She is impressed by the futility of attempting to remove oppression (or injustice) without understanding. The sacrifices and the disasters which come from a dream of *revolution*. And subsequent disillusionment. The need for an examination to try to discover whether it is possible to do anything at all.

But the model of 'science' is taken to be (a) physics (le mécanisme sociale, (b) Darwinism, biology. She does not develop any such 'science.' But her aim seems to be to give a *conceptual* analysis of "oppression" and of "political power" and "struggle for power," and of "freedom." This surely must be *prior* to any 'science' determining their "conditions of existence."

Galileo gave a definition of 'force' in mechanics: how to calculate, how to account for changes in the motions of bodies, how to account for changes in acceleration. But this is not what she wants to do. Although she speaks of making social activity similar to "un travail," her main aim is reaching *clarity* in *thinking*, in understanding. The methods of physics and of biology are not designed for this. (Compare what she herself says about science later on in this essay.) The changes in acceleration could themselves be *measured*; and the notion of 'force' fits in this context. But the idea of measuring "social changes" could hardly mean anything unless it were expressed in *statistical* data: changes in population, in average age of death, in the gross national product, and so forth.

She says there are "conditions of existence to which every society has to conform on pain of being either subdued or destroyed" (p. 59).[1] Do we know anything about these? "Without which society could not exist"—how do you know?

She speaks of "social necessities" (p. 60). It would be important to recognize that there are certain things which cannot be changed by political action, for instance. But she still seems to be using the phrase in the sense of "without which society could not exist."

"The existence of a particular *organism* (a frog, a dinosaur)," "the existence of a (any) *society*." Darwin was thinking of the existence of a *species*. Suppose someone said, "In those circumstances no society could exist": well suppose that a society ceases to exist—what is that like? We may know what is meant by saying that an organism has ceased to exist, or that a *species* has ceased to exist. But "all society would cease to exist" does not seem to mean there would be no human beings left alive. How would you know that a given society had ceased to exist? This is especially difficult where we do not allow for its being replaced by another—perhaps exterminated by conquest.

Marx saw oppression as a function of the development of productive forces. Simone Weil saw it as a function of the separation of those who direct (commanded) and those who carry out. The growth of technology, of specialization, the increasing separation between coordination or *management* (control) and *operation*. Bureaucratization in politics. Caught in "blind" developments which we do not understand. But this is not a scientific theory. The "advance of science," the "mastery of nature," has not meant a liberation of human persons, nor a liberation of the human spirit either.

"If you want to remove (or reduce) oppression, you have to know—and remove or meet—the conditions that give rise to it." There are reasons for holding that oppression is a feature of all states. But as far as Darwin and "conditions of existence" be concerned, there was nothing *inevitable* about the "evolution" of existing species. It just did go that way, that's all.

The loss of freedom, being the plaything of forces one does not understand: could this be said of everybody? Acting without understanding, without understanding the point of what one is doing. There is something in this. But it may lead to suggestions like "if you understand the necessity to which you are subject, you are free." The context of one's life is no longer in one's hands. This should have led her to see the difference between wage earners and slaves.

Does keeping control of my life depend on the exercise of *method*? If you can describe the masses and velocities of two bodies in collision, you can speak of what "inevitability" results. It is not like this with the consequences of a social organization or social development. Simone Weil realizes this: but says that *unless* we treat the consequences as "necessary," we cannot make sense of history; it must appear to have been a play of chance. Otherwise her position would be analogous to that of Marx in expecting the weakest section of society to become the most powerful while still remaining the weakest, that is, any move to reduce oppression would be impossible.

She speaks of "thinking" and of "mind" as something which cannot be produced by necessity, although theoretically it can be eliminated. And if the social organization *needs* or requires thinking, it is *forced* to grant some measure of initiative to individuals (a form of the limits to power from within the nature of the exercise of power). This does not mean that mind and thinking are not subject to necessity in *some* sense, although the idea of intellectual *force* is absurd.

If the idea of intellectual force is absurd, then the ways in which individuals influence one another in discussion, explanation, asking, teaching, and even propaganda cannot be described as the operation of *forces*. Although the consequences may be "out of our hands" and unwanted. Any teacher knows this. Socrates and Alcibiades.

Simone Weil's account in *L'Enracinement* is of ways in which the state is degrading. This is independent of "relations of production," even of the fact that it is bureaucratic—orders people about. This is a development of what she says in *Oppression and Liberty* (e.g. on p. 120). In the earlier work it is not so much the *exercise* of power as rather the *struggle* for power that makes liberty impossible. Compare: "The profound change in the economic struggle operates in the same direction; the State is incapable of constructing, but owing to the fact that it concentrates in its hands the most powerful means of coercion, it is brought, as it were, by its very weight gradually to become the central element when it comes to conquering and destroying" (p. 115).[2] Again compare: "The present social system provides no means of action other than machines for crushing humanity; whatever may be the intentions of those who use them, these machines crush and will continue to crush as long as they exist" (p. 119).[3]

One of the ways in which state influence is degrading is by creating the *illusion* of importance among all sections of the population. This is one reason why people, including Simone Weil, have wished they might *understand* the course of history—so as not to feel helpless in the face of it.

Both Marx and Simone Weil disregard national differences, differences between one culture and another, and differences of history. They wrote of oppression which comes from (or with) social organization as such. Not simply that they were describing *general* features of social organization—no matter what the national peculiarities might be. They wrote as though national (cultural) differences do not count, as though they do not have to be considered in writing of liberty and oppression. Simone Weil had changed her view by the time of *L'Enracinement*. And she was no longer thinking of "political action" as a form of *travail* or of *engineering*. She spoke of "needs of the soul": what the individual needs from the community without which it suffocates.

What is one to make of the various (repeated) attempts—and hopes—to throw off oppression (political oppression especially), to recreate a society of free men? If we say that they failed, is this like a failure in an engineering project or a military campaign? "They did not know what they were doing. They were acting blindly." But at least it was not like the fruitless efforts to cure someone of a disease, for there we should know the symptoms we would get rid of, and we should know what was meant by *cure*: we know what a body in good health is like. We know the "conditions of existence" which would have to be maintained.

If we speak of oppression and social injustice as a *malady*, nevertheless, this is not the same sort of problem. For one thing, nobody is interested in preserving or maintaining whatever it is in the man's body which prevents his recovery. How would you try to stop or prevent the unjust treatment of one individual by another individual? (Perhaps an extortionate moneylender. But better examples.) Probably not by trying to discover the "causes" of the unjust behaviour. If the problem is how to stop the injustice, this is not a *medical* problem.

Does one know what is meant by "la bonne volonté éclairée" (the enlightened goodwill) in this connexion (see p. 60)? It is misleading to speak of "le pouvoir" (power) as though it were an unambiguous *general* term, as she does: "Power, by definition, is only a means; or to put it better, to possess a power is simply to possess means of action which exceed the very limited force that a single individual has at his disposal" (p. 69).[4] The confusion here is that power is "only a means," and yet she says that men are prepared to sacrifice *everything else* to it.

If we do distinguish 'ends' and 'means' in the quasi-absolute way she intends, then power has become an end. To say that it is "essentially" or "in itself" a means suggests that there are some things which are by nature ends and others by nature means. I do not think sense can be made of this. Least of all in connexion with morality or human conduct.

Her model, no doubt, is the way in which, in modern industry, men exist for the sake of the machines—to serve the needs of the machines—rather than vice versa. "Hence one is brought face to face with a paradoxical situation, namely, that there is a method in the motions of work, but none in the mind of the worker. It would seem as though the method had transferred its abode from the mind into the matter" (p. 92).[5]

If one does emphasize this, then it can be misleading to use the term *mechanism* as she does when she speaks of "the mechanism of oppression," for instance. Her point is that the oppression is independent of individual decisions, individual wills.

NOTES

From Notes dated 18.2.68 and 24.2.68.

1. "Les conditions d'existence auxquelles toute société doit se conformer sous peine d'être ou subjuguée ou anéantie." *Oppression et Liberté*, p. 83.

2. "La transformation profonde de la lutte économique joue dans le même sens; l'État est incapable de construire, mais du fait qu'il concentre entre ses mains les moyens de contrainte les plus puissants, il est amené en quelque sorte part son poids même à devenir peu à peu l'élément central là où il s'agit de conquérir et de détruire." Ibid., p. 151.

3. "La société actuelle ne fournit pas d'autres moyens d'action que des machines à écraser l'humanité; quelles que puissent être les intentions de ceux qui les prennent an main, ces machines écrasent et écraseront aussi longtemps qu'elles existeront." Ibid., p. 155–56.

4. "Le pouvoir, par définition, ne constitue qu'un moyen; ou pour mieux dire posséder un pouvoir, cela consiste simplement à posséder des moyens d'action qui dépassent la force si restreinte dont un individu dispose par lui-même." Ibid., p. 95.

5. "Dès lors on se trouve en présence d'une situation paradoxale; à savoir qu'il y a de la méthode dans les mouvements du travail, mais non pas dans la pensée du travailleur. On dirait que la méthode a transféré son siège de l'esprit dans la matière." Ibid., p. 123.

CHAPTER FOUR

THE NEED FOR ROOTS

UPROOTEDNESS

A study of the first three sections of *The Need for Roots* ought to help one to see what she means by *uprootedness* through noticing that it may take so many forms. For I doubt if she wishes only to speak of so many different *causes* of uprootedness. She thinks that the different forms have something important in common with one another. And this is presumably what accounts for—or does something to account for—the ways in which rootlessness in one people or in one section of a people may beget rootlessness in another. What is more interesting and perhaps more obscure is why it is that a people or a society which is rooted does not give rise to rootlessness in those with whom it has contact.

Simone Weil does not speak of an *individual* as being rooted or rootless. I do not know whether she would think the term inapplicable in the same sense to individuals and to societies. She evidently does think that individuals are affected by the corruption when it does hit the society in which they live.

Rootedness has something to do with being able to find (spiritual) nourishment from the society in which one is living. Being able to grow, or continue the growth of what is already in growth there. Compare John Anderson: "When an individual is caught up in a movement, he may be kindled by a spirit which he did not originate." This is especially clear in artistic movements, scientific movements and religious movements. But Anderson often writes as though he were speaking of a system of mechanics, considering the mathematical or mechanical relations

31

between 'forces', and calculating the outcome of their interaction, which may be considered independently of place and of time, of territory or historical antecedents.

This is one of the questions which is impressing Simone Weil here, and it is one of the differences between her discussion in this book and the discussion in *Oppression and Liberty*. When she wrote the earlier essay, she would not have recognized so clearly culture, freedom, and perhaps 'salut' (well-being), to be dependent on or tied up with: to be the *product* or the *fruit* of the lives of these people there at this time. Something which cannot be predicted by any "law of motion of society" or in any way comparable to that in which phenomena of astronomy may be predicted.

In one sense she clearly thinks that uprootedness is the same phenomenon when it is studied in ancient history or in modern. The sense of being cut off, of having no part in the life of the society on which one is dependent. Unemployment as one of the forms of uprootedness.

"Participating in a life of the spirit"—"having a life of the spirit"—means participating in the life and *the language* of a society. (Think of language as something like *shoes*, which you would not need if you were just being yourself.) But if this is necessary, it is not sufficient. For what we call the deadening—or the death—of the spirit takes place in society too, and is not intelligible without reference to it. Destroying roots, rotting the roots: cutting off all nutrient, all spiritual food. This is connected with the destruction of all "spontaneous" or "original" motives. Contrast the desire for money. Malheur which leaves the sufferer *not* wanting rest and quiet in which to recover, but:

> Don't let us imagine that being worn out, all they will ask for is a comfortable existence. Nervous exhaustion caused by some recent misfortune makes it impossible for those concerned to settle down to enjoy a comfortable existence. It forces people to seek forgetfulness, sometimes in a dizzy round of exacerbated enjoyment—as was the case in 1918—at other times in some dark and dismal fanaticism. When misfortune bites too deeply, it creates a disposition towards misfortune, which makes people plunge headlong into themselves dragging others along with them.[1]

He who has roots has originality. *Because* he can draw nourishment from the society in which he lives (because there are matters which he can bring to other people: new ideas and ideas from them) opening up new fields which he had not known. New possibilities in friendship and in the lives of the people. Money, on the other hand, makes one look on people as opportunities or as markets: "The arts are dead, love is an attitude. . . ." (There is only one currency. . . .) We cannot even learn from our heritage. What makes it possible to learn from our heritage—to learn what greatness is, and what tragedy is, for instance—this is also what makes it possible to learn from other people.

Dependence on other people: servility. Is not this what the preoccupation with money encourages? 'Security': fear of anything which is unsettling. Innovation only when it helps to reduce costs, and so forth. Nothing important on its own account except the Gross National Product. In seeking money I am doing nothing which will give growth to the spiritual life of anyone. Payment—*size* of payment, figures, *nominal* wage or salary—as a sign of *status*. *Differentials*. Compare Kierkegaard: "Be proud, if you must (though it were better if you were not). But in God's name, do not be proud of money; for there is nothing which so degrades a man" (*Either/Or*). "Equality of esteem." Income as a sign of esteem. This can be contrasted with the equality which comes from "nakedness of spirit."

The Labour Party's "equality of esteem" is a perversion or caricature of this. The "esteem" is "What people think of you"—sham grandeur. The obsession with "snobbery" goes with this. "Everyone should be treated in the same way," that is, as regards payment, holidays, schools attended, and so on. In this way there is no consideration of des êtres humains comme tels (human beings like these). The growth of "public ownership" seems to go with a *decline* of respect for public property—parks, public buildings, and transport. (Why is this?)

Social Forces

Simone Weil sometimes writes of "la force" (or "la nécessité") as though it were *a* force: something by which human actions (and thoughts) are impelled. This comes out most sharply when she wants to distinguish between the operation of *la pesanteur* and the operation of *la grâce*. The difficulty is in making the comparison here: as though we could distinguish between those motions which are "due to gravity" and those which are "due to grace." As though "due to gravity" were like saying "due to the impact of such and such a body of such mass, with such velocity, from such a direction." As we might distinguish between what is due to gravity and what is due to impact or fruition. Or (in plants) between what is due to gravity and what is due to light.

When we speak of gravity, we speak of the *kind* of influence of one body on another (one motion on another). But "due to grace" does not seem to have a *parallel* generality, because we cannot refer to laws which are expressions or illustrations of what we mean by 'grace', as we can when we speak of gravitation. Simone Weil would not admit this: she thought there could be a "science" of grace or supernatural influence. And she seemed to think of this science as modelled on physics. Compare *Oppression and Liberty*: "The true knowledge of social mechanics implies that of the conditions under which the supernatural operation of an infinitely small quantity of pure good, placed at the right point, can neutralize gravity" (p. 167).[2]

This may be relevant to such questions as whether history is (should try to be) a science, the advantages or disadvantages of speaking of "social forces" when discussing the exercise of political power, oppression and liberty, and various forms of constraint. But compare also *Oppression and Liberty*: "To these it is given to feed on a good which, being situated outside this world, is not subject to any social influence whatever" (p. 157).[3] Here the explanatory phrase *looks* like an explanation for physical things "outside the influence of gravity."

In *The Need for Roots* she emphasizes much more the ways in which human beings (or human spirits) may be *nourished* by the society in which they live and move: that a liberation *from* the "collectivité" would not make the human soul more active, but would leave it empty.

In considering "the role of ideas in history," or "the role (if any) of ideas in action," one may wish to distinguish in a *general* way between "what is due to force" and "what is due to thought": the image of 'thought' or 'thinking' as a kind of *process* which may come in conflict with other processes and influences or may be overridden by them. But if we try to understand the relations of human beings to one another, or their relations to institutions (industry, government, education . . .), or their relations to historical developments, we cannot get far by trying to think of them as we might of bodies, solid or fluid, in a conglomerate. The problems are not of this sort, and if we speak of 'influence', the word has a different grammar here. "Spiritual servitude consists in confusing the necessary with the good" (p. 165).[4] She often makes "l'opération surnaturelle du bien joui" (the benefit of the supernatural operation of goodness) coincide with the establishment (and preservation?) of "equilibrium." (Does she use 'equilibrium' in an almost *absolute* sense? Should we not say "in equilibrium relative to so and so"?)

What is meant by "being in the world" and by "not being in the world"? If one speaks of "les forces morales" as stemming from or being "le surnaturel"—what is this saying? Does it refer to a way of *explaining* moral motives? Or to what weighs in moral reasonings—what are grounds or reasons in connexion with moral problems? It cannot be meant, of course, that "natural" circumstances and happenings never make any difference to the "right" solution of a moral problem.

In *Oppression and Liberty* she says: "moral phenomena . . . are not subject to physical necessity, but they are subject to necessity" (p. 178).[5]

I do not understand *soumis* (subject to) here, even in connexion with "les phénomènes physiques." I can understand "being subjected to such and such pressure" or "being subjected to radiation of such and such a sort," but being subjected to *necessity*? *What* is subject to necessity? Can one *describe* the phenomena as they are and are "then" subjected to necessity? "This rod was subjected to such and such strains when it was made a part of this bridge (or of this machine)." Someone might say it is *logical* necessity in both cases. But does Simone Weil want to say this? How does she *discover* the necessity of 'thought'? How does one distinguish between what follows of necessity and what does not? And when a thought (or physical phenomenon) does follow another "by necessity," its happening (or following) is not *due* to necessity; rather that expression—this happening was due to that—is the *expression* of necessity. In all this discussion she hardly distinguishes between "cause and effect" and "ground and consequent." On the other hand, on page 235 she emphasises *labour, attitude to labour,* and so forth. This is one of the most valuable points in her discussions.

ROOTEDNESS

In the Marxian conception of 'social structure' and in Simone Weil's conception of 'social organization': as though there were one fundamental structure or organization of a society and it were sensible to ask what *the* social structure of this or that society is, and as though the only important difference between one society and another would lie (could not but lie) in the relations of production, which are thought then to determine other features of the life in that society.

The crippling abstraction in the "theoretical description of a free society" and similarly in the conception of a free life as a life in which a man's activities are guided by his own thinking, and especially in her conception of *thinking* and of the relation between thinking and action. The relation between thinking and manual labour: she conceives of this too exclusively in terms of the relation between method and the application of it in the carrying out of an engineering operation.

She thinks here of the distinction of oppression and liberty in terms of (or by reference to?) the degree to which an individual does not have to act in any way for which he cannot understand the reason. Acting from understanding, in this sense.

When she came to write *The Need for Roots*, she was more impressed by the evils that come from conquest, and the oppression there is when one population is subjugated by a foreign conqueror. It was in this connexion that she recognized how important its *past* is to any people.

People live in a culture they have inherited. This does not mean that their past history is all, or even mostly, a cause for congratulation. But it is this from which their present way of living and present institutions have grown. And it is in terms of this that they understand life; it is as though the past history and traditions were the language in which the big problems now facing us are formulated; it is in terms of this that we understand problems, or recognize them, and new developments.

The difference between a culture and a past which is manifestly *theirs* and a culture which has been thrust upon them (history books which they are forced to recite, literature which they may be forced to recite without understanding, and so on).

In connexion with this Simone Weil recognized that whatever we call 'a society'—leaving aside for the moment the distinction between a society and the state—is something different from organization for production.

One might imagine a group of people engaged on some engineering project and each of them understanding the activities of the others in this connexion, but nevertheless being from as many different countries, as many different cultures and traditions themselves, as there were people. (Compare prisoners of war; immigrants in the U.S.A.) And the fact that they were joining in this common activity would not make them members of a society in the sense in which one commonly uses that phrase. The point here is to bring out the fact that we do speak of "a society" in a different sense from any which this construction would satisfy.

And further: people who belong to the same society, who are Londoners or Englishmen or Welshmen or Frenchmen, are not ipso facto engaged in some common work of production. (The dangers of nationalism and doctrinaire exclusiveness.)

Her earlier view (a rational order of production) left no room for, did not take account of, a great deal of what does characterize "belonging to a particular society."

But further: even the question of what it could mean to "make the value of manual labour central in a society" and what overcoming or removing the conditions of labour which make it servile, or the possibility of manual labour that was not servile: this is one of the big problems for her all her life, as it had been also for Marx. She sees now that more belongs to this than simply, say, having the status of skilled craftsman and being able to understand the enterprises on which one is engaged. The conception of 'servile labour', in fact, could not be separated from the conception of the *proletariate*. This same point is probably one of the features of Marxist doctrine that was important, although Marx does not make it at all clear.

You cannot give a satisfactory account of what makes manual workers into a proletariate (in the sense in which Marx speaks of this) either by reference to their low and inadequate wages, or by reference to the "alienation of labour" alone, or by reference to the working conditions. All of these are important. But you cannot describe the proletariate by describing simply the conditions of workers in their direct relation to the productive process.

I repeat that these questions are important. But they leave the question still unanswered of what there is that is degrading or degraded about the condition of the proletariate. This is what Simone Weil discusses in terms of le déracinement ouvrier (the worker's uprootedness). She is able to give a similar sort of discussion of the conditions of peasants or farm workers which Marxists so commonly neglected.

So the notion of servility has a great deal more to it, and cannot be described in as simple terms as we find in the earlier essay.

Her emphasis on the evil which generally results from conquest by a foreign power—her placing of this evil in what she calls déracinement—this was something to which she seems to have come in revising her earlier reasons for pacifism. She was now clear as to where the evil of conquest would lie.

This went with a much less abstract account of societies, and especially of the relation between *state* and citizens. This was something of which her earlier essay had hardly made an important point any more than Marx does. Marxists and also Simone Weil regard the exercise of state power as though it were very much the same thing as the exercise of economic power. And one reason for this is that neither of them takes very seriously the relations *between* states. (Lenin had done something to develop this in his *Imperialism*. But he treats economic imperialism as fundamental; political imperialism, political demands, and so on, are an extension of economic imperialism and demands. There is no thought that political *domination* might be something else. This is one of the reasons why, in Lenin as well as in Marx, the notion of war and of conquest is neglected—treated almost as a detail which can be put into proper shape when we have time. Compare Lenin's curious admiration for Clausewitz's saying.)

One reason why Simone Weil asked later, "Is there a Marxist doctrine?" may have been that she now recognized that the consideration of "relations of production" and "the division between intellectual and manual labour" do not give an adequate starting point nor suggest a method for an account of the proletariate or of "social oppression."

Conquest has often changed the character of states, not only those which are annexed, but the character of those which are thereby extended.

Here we seem to have a connexion between the notion of a 'state' and the notion of a 'country'. Simone Weil goes into a long discussion of the relations between patriotism and the state (or "service of the state").

But all of this is part of a general method of treating social questions: the method which is underlined by the way in which *The Need for Roots* begins. The discussion of what she calls "the needs of the soul."

Here again is the discussion of the relation of the individual to *la collectivité*. But she now sees this as something much more complicated and is not content to sketch a kind of opposition of contrast between the social organization and the individual.

With regard to the expression "the needs of the soul": this has nothing to do with an idea of "self-fulfilment." It is not the needs of the *writer's* soul—the needs of my soul—which are important here, but rather the needs of the soul of anyone with whom I am concerned. This is why she begins with the reference to duties, and why she calls the whole book "a prelude to a declaration of duties to human beings." (Notice that it is not duties to the state.)

Liberty: "the loss of which robs life of its value." She need not have retracted this when she wrote *The Need for Roots*. But the *loss* can happen in more ways than one.

She lays the emphasis now more upon the soul's finding nourishment—partly getting stimulus from, learning from, getting inspiration, and, nota bene, *energy*.

The point in common with the earlier essay might be: that without the nourishment the individual is not able to act. Perhaps the notion of "having the course of his life in his own hands" would suggest a life that comes from him. But nothing will come from him if the soul has not the nourishment it needs. And what she emphasizes here is that the nourishment itself does *not* come from him (and generally he cannot provide it or secure it).

This gives new importance to the question of *how* the individual is related to the collectivity. Again we might ask what sort of study this is. And again we should notice that these are not questions a sociologist would ask.

She now considers special historical circumstances, special historical developments, as she had not in the earlier essay; her general discussion is much further from sociology than the earlier one was.

This brings out something of the character of political philosophy.

In the whole conception of the needs of the soul and its relation to "duties towards human beings" we have to do with judgments of value. Judgments of value enter in complicated ways all through her discussion.

The very extent to which she gives an historical account of the origin of the modern notion of the 'State' which she ascribed to Richelieu (whether this is historically accurate or not is not the main point here) makes it plain that she is not writing a work on history. The historical account is part of an attempt to come to terms with a philosophical problem. And as far as she is concerned, this philosophical problem is also a practical problem.

Parallel between the circumstances in 1943 and the situation of Israel preparing to return to Palestine after the captivity. (What do we mean when we say that those two tribes kept their identities, and that the others were "lost"?)

The relation of Frenchmen to their country (la patrie, patriotism) on the one hand, their relation to the State on the other.

This discussion again brings in criteria and problems that are different from those of sociologists.

She does not try to formulate a definition of the 'state'. But the distinction of state and country is important.

There are common dangers, and so common problems, facing all the passengers and crew involved in a shipwreck. But for one thing, these are not problems symbolising the past or more distant future. Not problems about the character of the society and the survival of *that*.

The notion of having roots and the notion of feeling at home (se sentent chez eux). This seems to be a condition for recognizing other people as being members of the same society. And as having common responsibilities. Some idea *allied* to that of communication, and more especially to that of speaking a common language: a common life. Recognizing common responsibilities and common *problems*. Economic problems would be among them, but consider problems in the threat from a foreign aggressor. The idea of what is foreign and what is not.

Her problem is: how France can be brought alive again—how it can start a new life after the German occupation. This notion of the life of the society and of the decline, the ruin, and death of a society (not the same as the death of all those living there), as contrasted with a life in which there are problems, in a sense that is somewhat analogous to that in which there are problems in the life of a human being—problems which are not simply theoretical ones.

This is the kind of conception that is vital for her. And it is with a view to understanding society in this sense that she carries out her inquiries.

Whether a sociologist has ever been, or ever would be interested in this sort of inquiry?

The above phrase "comes from him": as "thinking comes from him." Compare Wittgenstein's emphasis on "speaking in the first person" when discussing ethics. And also, his emphasis on *Ursprünglichkeit* (naturalness, simplicity).

"But freedom is of course another word for subjectivity, and if some fine day she does not hold out any longer, some time or other she despairs of the possibility of being creative out of herself and seeks shelter and security in the objective" (Thomas Mann, *Doctor Faustus*, trans. H. T. Lowe-Porter, London: Secker and Warburg, 1951, p. 190).[6]

NOTES

From Notes dated 26.2.64; undated notes;
Notes dated 19.12.67 and Notes dated 29.4.68.

1. *The Need for Roots*, trans. A. F. Wills, London: Routledge and Kegan Paul, 1952, pp. 92–3.

"Qu'on n'image pas qu'étant épuisés ils ne demanderont que le bien-être. L'épuisement nerveux causé par un malheur récent empêche de s'installer dans le bien-être. Il contraint à chercher l'oubli, soit dans une soûlerie de jouissances exaspérées—comme ce fut le cas après 1918—soit dans quelque sombre fanatisme. Le malheur qui a mordu trop profondément suscite une disposition au malheur qui contraint à y précipiter soi-même et autrui." Simone Weil, *L'Enracinement*, Paris: Gallimard, 1949, p. 126.

2. "La véritable connaissance de la mécanique sociale implique celle des conditions auxquelles l'opération surnaturelle d'une quantité infiniment petite de bien pur, placée au point convenable, peut neutraliser la pesanteur." *Oppression et Liberté*, p. 218.

3. "A ceux-là il est accordé de se nourrir d'un bien qui, étant situé hors de ce monde, n'est soumis à aucune influence sociale." Ibid., p. 206.

4. "L'asservissement spirituel consiste dans la confusion du nécessaire et du bien." Ibid., p. 216.

5. "Les phénomènes moraux . . . ne sont pas soumis à la nécessité physique, mais ils sont soumis à la nécessité." Ibid., p. 234.

6. "Aber Freiheit ist ja ein anderes Wort für Subjektivität, und eines Tages hält die es nicht mehr mit sich aus, irgendwann verzweifelt sie an der Möglichkeit, von sich aus schöpferisch zu sein, und sucht Schutz und Sicherheit beim Objektiven." Thomas Mann, *Doktor Faustus*, Frankfurt: Fischer, 1967, p. 253.

PART TWO

Science and Necessity

CHAPTER FIVE

THE WORLD AND NECESSITY

To say that the world is governed by "necessity," in the singular, as if in analogy to "all physical operations are subject to entropy," or "obey the second law of thermodynamics": as a statement in the philosophy of science, these would show bad confusions. The idea that "matter" shows "complete passivity" and consequently "complete obedience." Once again, in the ordinary sense of these expressions, this is meaningless.

Descartes's notion of geometrical bodies: application of mathematical methods to nature? But we also have the Pythagorean view. It would be *stupid* to say that the Pythagoreans were mistaken in speaking about mathematics as they did. Simone Weil *seems* to say that the only true physics is pure mathematics.

But what of the criticisms by Parmenides and by Plato? Why does she ignore this? They insisted, roughly, that what form of existence things have depends on whether we can give an account of this.

Plato turned to myths in his dialogues. I do not know why he did this. But it might have been to avoid trying to do what Simone Weil is trying to do here. Speaking of the world in relation to the will of God.

I want to explain *the kind* of difficulty I have with Simone Weil's language.

The difficulty of understanding the poetry of a country even when you "can speak the language." Or the music of another culture or tradition (say Indian music). I am sure I understand hardly anything of such translations as I have read from Buddhist or Hindu religious writings. But the idea of an analogy here may be a mirage, for, in regard to poetry and music, anyway, I am expressing a long familiarity with the way such people live and with the significance which such expressions or gestures or cadences have for them. I do not know how much of this has analogues in my trouble with Simone Weil's way of speaking.

When Weil turns to folklore, finding parallels in different folk tales, and also between them and doctrines of Christianity—how is this different from Plato's myths? (She seems to suggest that the Pythagoreans were expressing the same ideas in geometry.) Ways in which people come to conceive or express their relation to the world, and their situation—la condition humaine (their lives are ruled by material forces, and they aspire to justice).

Plato turned to myths when it was (or seemed to be) a question of how the world was brought about, of the course of souls after death, and also when it was a question of "explaining" the destinies of men on earth—why they are born at these times or places, there and thus—and why they lead these and these lives, others different lives, and so on. (The "choice of lives" in *Republic* X.)

But perhaps a closer parallel is the idea of the composition of the World Soul in the *Timaeus*, or the idea of a world soul altogether. If we call this a myth, it is different, has a different function, from the myths at the end of the *Phaedo* or the *Gorgias* and the *Republic*; more akin, perhaps, to that of the *Phaedrus*. See "God in Plato": "The soul is not the voῦς. It is the engendered God who is related to the creation as *mediator*, at the intersection of the other world and this world."[1]

Time as a likeness of eternity, moving according to number ("Schematism of the Categories"?) The possibility of discourse.

But here Plato's language is *openly* figurative: and we may ask what it is he is wanting to see, what he is trying to suggest. He is not using language which looks as though it *might* be meant to apply to empirical inquiry. And we are not inclined to criticise it as though it were part of an empirical inquiry or discussion. Or as though it were an account (explanation) of the concepts used in empirical science.

There are special reasons why Simone Weil does what she does. She has not started with the figures of the Demiourgos, the intelligible model, and "all that was visible." She is not addressing the same problems (εἴδωλον, μεθέξις) (image, participation). She does not want to speak of "a completely true" account with which the account given in theoretical science (even with the idea of "une véritable science") is to be contrasted. Her emphasis is on *Amour* de la réalité in a way that does not come into Plato's discourse.

Weil uses the expression 'connaissance du monde' (knowledge of the world), which I hardly follow. She thinks both Greek and Classical science aimed at this, the difference being in what they wanted to include in the connaissance: classical science was less complete. But I wonder if the word has the same sense at all when you speak of "une connaissance du monde" and when you speak of knowledge of some important point in solid-state physics.

World Soul: Weil sees this idea as that of the son of God making the "point of intersection" of God and the world. The way she speaks in *Intimations of Christianity* of *necessity* and of *consent* to necessity is the same idea: the contemplation of necessity given in the contemplation of affliction, and κατ ἐξοχήν (par excellence) in the crucifixion.

For some reason, the *universality* of this necessity, and so of the possibility of comparable affliction, was important to her. This necessity and this possibility belong to la misère humaine or to la condition humaine and so to creation.

That it is through necessity that one comes close to God—in affliction one comes close to God—this is the teaching of the Passion.

And so the idea of science as aspiring to a knowledge of the *world*, expressible in mathematical terms, was important to her. She does not ask (I think) whether anything like "an *image* of the world" plays any part in the acquisition of scientific knowledge: the solutions of problems in science. In *L'Enracinement* she remarks that gathering "knowledge" (facts) does not bring one nearer to *la réalité*. This is what is important: this notion of the relation of science to *la réalité*. The care for connaissance en sense scientifique du mort (knowledge of death in the scientific sense) would only be a necessary condition.

But this knowledge—the discovery of logos, the revelation of necessity—would not be a step nearer to *reality* without *amour*. This is why this later and apparently strange view of her later writings is necessary for the conception of *science* (une science véritable) as well. (There is still the difficult conception of l'amour du *monde*.)

She speaks of *la* réalité, in the singular, almost as though there could be no question about this. And as though "contact with reality" always meant the same thing, or perhaps that there is some one sense which is the fundamental one.

In "The causes of liberty and oppression," we already find a recognition of universality there, but only in regard to matter (la matière). The point is chiefly that both oppressors and oppressed are governed in what they do by "le mécanisme sociale." *Oppression and Liberty*: "Every judgement bears upon an objective set of circumstances, and consequently upon a warp and woof of necessities. Living man can on no account cease to be hemmed in on all sides by an absolutely inflexible necessity; but since he is a thinking creature, he can choose between either blindly submitting to the spur with which necessity pricks him on from outside, or else adapting himself to the inner representation of it that he forms in his own mind; and it is in this that the contrast between servitude and liberty lies" (pp. 85–86).[2]

When a man is subject, not only to material forces, but to human wills (the society in which he lives), his condition is worse, since he cannot apply "la pensée" to an understanding of those human wills, as he can to matter and motion. "To the extent to which a man's fate is dependent on other men, his own life escapes not only out of his hands, but also out of the control of his intelligence" (p. 96).[3]

In her *Fragments*, London 1943, later in the same volume, Weil says, "It is not his body alone that is thus subject, but all his thoughts as well" (p. 159).[4] And in "Is There a Marxist Doctrine?" she says, "moral phenomena . . . are not subject to physical necessity, but they are subject to necessity" (p. 178).[5] This belongs to 1943; and these remarks are in line with what she was saying about "la pesanteur morale" (moral gravity).

In the essay on the *Iliad* she has already come near to the later view (it was written apparently in 1939–1940). But this essay is also in many respects in line with the view of "Les causes de la liberté et l'oppression" that both oppressors and oppressed are victims of or subject to le mécanisme sociale.

The big difference between "The causes of liberty and oppression" and, for example, *Intuitions Pré-Chrétiennes* is that in the earlier essay there is not the same relation between necessity and intelligence; it is not described as the relation of what is contemplated to the contemplation of it. (There is no such role of contemplation at all.)

Perhaps this is not in the essay on the *Iliad* either. But there we do have the emphasis on *compassion*: the compassion shown in the portrayal of the contestants involved in the war. This is something which makes it a poem which could not have been written by the early Hebrews. And in a sense, I suppose, this requires a detachment. It is taking a point of view which is not identified with the desire for victory or for glory, and especially, one which is free from contempt.

But it is still something very different from the love of necessity *itself*.

Nor do we have an identification of the force or necessity to which the warriors are subject with the "conditional necessity" of mathematics. And so there is not the emphasis upon the mean proportional and upon mediation.

In "The causes of liberty and oppression" the treatment is much more in accordance with *Republic* 493, with an emphasis on the opposition between necessity and the good.

Perhaps it would be said that this opposition is recognized in the later religious treatment as well, in so far as she sees necessity as a feature of *Creation* (or the created world) which is "negation" of God (who is identified with Good). All right. But the identification of necessity with mathematical necessity is not Plato's view in the *Timaeus*.

It seems as though her religious views were a development from the Newtonian mechanical view of the world—or the material world—and also a development from the Marxist view: vide the letter to Bernanos.

But I think it is possible that she falls into a confusion over senses of 'dependence': of causal dependence, moral dependence, and religious dependence.

NOTES

From undated Notes and Notes dated 3.12.68.

1. "God in Plato," *On Science, Necessity and the Love of God*, ed. and trans. Richard Rees, London: Oxford University Press, p. 135.

"L'âme n'est pas νοῦς. C'est le Dieu engendré dans son rapport avec la création, à l'intersection de l'autre monde et de celui-ci, comme *médiateur*," Simone Weil, *La Source Grecque*, Paris: Gallimard, 1953, p. 124.

2. "Tout jugement porte sur une situation objective, et par suite sur un tissu de nécessités. L'homme vivant ne peut en aucun cas cesser d'être enserré de toutes parts par une nécessité absolument inflexible; mais comme il pense, il a le choix entre céder aveuglément à l'aiguillon par lequel elle le pousse de l'extérieur, ou bien se conformer à la représentation intérieure qu'il s'en forge; et c'est en quoi consiste l'opposition entre servitude et liberté." *Oppression et Liberté*, p. 115.

3. "Dans la mesure où le sort d'un homme dépend d'autres hommes, sa propre vie échappe non seulement à ses mains, mais aussi à son intelligence." Ibid., p. 127.

4. "Ce n'est son corps seul qui est ainsi soumis, mais aussi toutes ses pensées." Ibid., p. 209.

5. "Les phénomènes moraux . . . ne sont pas soumis à la nécessité physique, mais ils sont soumis à la nécessité." Ibid., p. 234.

CHAPTER SIX

THOUGHT, NECESSITY, AND CONTEMPLATION

THE WORLD AS OBSTACLE

In the *Leçons de Philosophie* the grasp or 'constatation' of reality came primarily through producing transformations, either experimentally in a laboratory or in practical affairs; in other words, it came by acting upon things and obstacles; for this view, classical science or mechanics would have given a much more adequate account of what a representation of the world could be. Le monde comme obstacle (the world as obstacle).

This is the necessity expressed in the laws of mechanics. But Weil hardly distinguishes between what one might call the necessity of any actual happening, which might be explained by the laws of mechanics, on the one hand, and the necessity of the conclusion of a mathematical proof (or any formal inference) on the other. She emphasised the role of deduction in connection with experiments, but she hardly examines the difference between establishing a conclusion by experiment and reaching a conclusion by deduction. Her phrase 'infinite error' suggests that they are not comparable, and also that the error is not even theoretically corrigible. But then it is not what we'd call an *error* at all. She emphasises the role of ideal cases and closed systems and mechanical models in connection with experiments. But she says hardly anything about questions of evidence, sufficient evidence, and insufficient evidence. And it would seem that it is something like a miracle, astonishing, that we can make predictions on these formal criteria, employ calculations and find

51

the results of actual happenings approximately in accordance with them, although neither numbers nor anything like mathematical operations belong to the processes themselves. How can anything except a mathematical operation be *like* a mathematical operation? What sort of "accordance" is this—the relation between the ideal and the actual description—this is left out.

She says that "l'idéal de l'expérience est donné par la déduction" (*Leçons*, p. 113) (the ideal of the experiment is given by the deduction) on the ground that in the experiment one seeks to create a closed system. I do not think this is true, if it means that one does not recognise that the result, even when "irrelevant circumstances" have been excluded, may be of one sort or it may be of another.

"The ideal of the experiment is given by the deduction":

> Induction can be thought of as an application of the principle: "Relationships which recur often can be thought of as constant." In induction, there is a purely mechanical factor, habit, but one also assumes that this constant character of events is a sign of necessity. Since this necessity is something that we have assumed to exist, and have not established that it does exist, we have recourse to an elaboration of hypotheses. (*Lectures on Philosophy*, pp. 105–106)[1]

As though experiments were a kind of poor substitute for deduction. (Perhaps more importantly, if we *think* that deduction is what we should like to have, we deceive ourselves. The deduction would not be a discovery.)

In any case, Weil thinks of necessity, and of the employment of method, as belonging to *action*—action méthodique. It is only here that we can be said to be *thinking*. This action would include experimenting and perhaps the actual performance of calculations.

She seems to have thought of the application of the ideal cases, the comparison of the perfect case and the imperfect case, as though it were hardly different from the comparison of greater and lesser perfection among actual cases. And this would go along with her view that a conclusion from an experiment is simply an imperfect form of what would be perfect if we had a deduction.

Relations of thought and reality are shown especially in the relations between thought (method) and action. What does not come from pure thought, what appears as an *obstacle* is reality.

Sometimes she uses 'reality' and 'necessity' in ways that are nearly synonymous. Water won't flow uphill. I have contact with reality (the world) when I am producing transformations in it. I can understand transformations in things and processes when I can produce them, construct them.

Gaining control of—being able to cope with—things and *understanding* them go hand in hand. I can then see the necessity in what happens. I am able to construct (or reconstruct) transformations in so far as these transformations can be reduced to (and constructed from) motions, complexes of motion.

To understand all things in terms of motion is the aim or standpoint of mechanics. It is by interpreting things in mechanical terms that we show their relation to thought (method, understanding). So long as I am *passive*, I have no sense either of space or of time (the necessities of space and the necessities of time). I have a sense of them only when I am engaged in projects.

There is still the difference between the *image*, or model of the world as a complete or closed system, and the *reality* "qui nous dépasse infiniment" (pp. 106, 107) ("which infinitely transcends us," *Lectures*, III). It is a *reality* for us in so far as we encounter it as something not given in the system.

To think of the world as created by God, and to think of everything as intelligible to an understanding, that is, as constructible, these come to much the same thing. This is superficial, and not what Weil would have taught six years later.

Order depends on our having language, if only because language makes it possible for us to recognize temporal sequence. "Order is something which unfolds in time, and depends on a relationship between successive operations. Without language there is no recollection: so, an operation which has taken place would no longer exist" (*Lectures*, p. 69).[2]

In her earlier view, up to 1934 or 1935, anyway, she emphasised the relation and the contrast between what we have through *language* and what we have through *action* (bodily movement) especially in regard to our relations to things. In our actions, the relations which we have to things are determined by our needs. And we do not ourselves decide or determine what our needs shall be. This may be decided, for example, by the circumstances and the obstacles which I happen to meet. If I act from a need for food, I may find myself in danger, and driven by a need of another sort. My needs may determine what I experience in things, or what I find out about them. But there is no "objective" order in what I have in this way. "Les besoins se succèdent au hasard," *Leçons*, p. 53 ("Needs follow one another by chance," *Lectures*, p. 70).

NECESSITY

When Weil speaks, in *Intuitions Pré-Chrétiennes*, of conceiving of force as necessity, this reminds one of Plato's "conceiving of what is visible as intelligible" in the *Timaeus*. But she never raises the question of whether this can be done exhaustively, or whether there is, as Plato in the *Timaeus* suggested, some residue of necessity which cannot be seen as intelligible in the sense in which truths of geometry are intelligible.

What is important is, for one thing, that Weil now speaks of the *contemplation* of necessity, as she had not spoken in the *Leçons de Philosophie*. She had said there that the objective necessity which is given in order and method is independent of our needs, and therefore there is some difference between the grasp of order and "constatation." (This notion of 'constatation' is important in connection with learning by experiment.) But she had said, in the *Leçons de Philosophie*, that the order or the method comes *from us*. And she would have rejected this from 1940 onwards, when she said that the necessity recognized is neither friend nor enemy. Also—and this is important—that the love of necessity is not the love of other human beings (nor on account of them); this has to do with the *consent* to necessity, not just the recognition of it. It is important in connection with the love of the world, or amor fati (*Intuitions Pré-Chrétiennes*, p. 149). It is not out of love for other people that we consent to necessity. The love of other people is rather an obstacle to the consent. "The love of the world is not the love of any human person, and nevertheless is the love of something like a person."

There is no *reason* for loving "necessity," even after one has come to contemplation of it; or none outside beauty and recognizing that all beauty is beauty of the world.

Consent to necessity or love of necessity is possible through the supernatural part of the soul, or through supernatural virtue. She now speaks of the Stoic 'amor fati' and identifies the 'fatum' with 'la nécessité'. When she speaks of Marcus Aurelius in the lectures, I do not think she ascribed to him the view that amor fati is a supernatural virtue. (It hardly could have been something he would say anyway, because of what she calls there his "pantheism." If he was a pantheist, as she said he was, then 'supernatural' would not mean much.)

She does use the term 'force' in the *Leçons de Philosophie*, when she is speaking of Machiavelli (p. 157), saying that Machiavel fait une séparation complète entre la force et le droit, *Leçons*, p. 156. (Machiavelli made force and law completely separate from one another, *Lectures*, p. 152.) Perhaps it was by an extension of this conception of force in human affairs that she came to her later view, in the essay *The Iliad: A Poem of Force*, for example. She may have changed some of her views about the relation of la force and la nécessité. "The difference—distance—between la nécessité and le bien." Love of necessity because it is *not* God, but his creation.

Necessity, contemplation, and consent. In *Intuitions Pré-Chrétiennes* (p. 155) Weil speaks of the contemplation as "cette attention intellectuelle" (this intellectual attention). And she says that this can give rise (suscite) only to "une demi-réalité." She goes on to say that we confer on things and on beings about us, in so far as we are capable of it, the fullness of reality—"la plénitude de la réalité"—when we add to the "attention intellectuelle" the attention which is still superior to it and which is "acceptation, consentement, amour" (acceptance, consent, love)—those three being equivalent or synonymous in this context, apparently.[3]

Thus *reality* and *obstacle* are no longer identified; nor *reality* and *necessity* either.

The notion of a 'half-reality' is obscure. Is it half reality and half illusion? Not in the ordinary sense of 'illusion' anyway. Granting that there is more to be known or said about it, it does not follow that what we do know is unreal.

The idea of 'contact with reality', in connection with something one loves, is important. The connection between necessity and the love of God is that the love of God shows itself, appears, in the consent to, or love of, the world. (The obvious contrast between this and devotion to Mammon.)

Pantheism: the objection that Simone Weil's view is pantheism. Compare her criticisms of—remarks on—pantheism in the *Leçons*.

The reason why science is important, that is to say, physics is important, in connection with the love of God, is that it is in physics that the mathematical structure of the world, and in this way the world under the form of necessity, is shown.

Spinoza: seeing things under the form of eternity; compare also *facies totius univerai* (the face of the whole universe). Contemplating the whole world as subject to (mathematical) necessity.

To speak of "a *universal* necessity" would be misleading or confusing. For it suggests something like an all-embracing law (compare reference to "gravity"). Or it suggests that there is some common form, or common "mathematical connection" which is everywhere the same. I do not think there is justification for speaking so; and certainly no justification in physics.

Weil also wants to speak of *time* as the form of natural necessity. But what is mathematical here? She would agree with Spinoza in ruling out final causes as an "explanation of the world" (or interpretation of the world). But her earlier emphasis on time and action and on "l'imprévu" (the unforeseen) would give a sense to 'contingency' which Spinoza does not. And the Amour which *is* God is not something from which creation follows by logical necessity. Creation is rather a "denial" of God. (This way of putting it would have to be taken seriously.)

The phrase "intellectual love of God" is one which her remarks sometimes suggest; other remarks not at all. The reference to beauty which cannot be explained might count the other way.

"The beauty of a mathematical proof": I do not stand and contemplate a mathematical proof as I do a landscape. Nor listen to it as to a piece of music or a drama. "La beauté est une chose qui se mange" (beauty is something that consumes itself).

In *Intuitions Pré-Chrétiennes* Weil says: "There is an analogy between the faithfulness of a right-angled triangle to the relationship which prohibits it from leaving the circle whose diameter is the hypotenuse, and that of a man who refrains from acquiring power or money at the cost of a fraud, for example. The former could be seen as a perfect model of the latter."[4]

To speak of fidélité in both these cases is an example of Weil's use of a simile or metaphor with no clue as to what the precise meaning could be. It leaves on one side the obvious *differences* between 'impossibility' in mathematics, and 'impossibility' in moral alternatives: he rejects making money by fraud as unthinkable, not because he does not know what it would be like. I could *understand* someone who accused me of having done just that.

A part of this view is that causal relations among physical happenings—physical necessity, physical impossibility, dependence (of boiling point on atmospheric pressure), inevitability, and so forth—that these are *mathematical* relations. This enables Weil to take any regularity in physical happenings as a model of morally right action. (Compare Kantian legalism.) In other places she would say that the "obedience" of material happenings is *blind* to obedience. And this would not be a model for morality, on her view.

Compare Pensées sans ordre pp. 96 (infra) 97:

> The mechanism of necessity transposes itself unchanged at all levels in brute matter, plants, animals, people, souls. Looked at from our standpoint, from our perspective, it is totally blind. But if we transport our heart outside of ourselves, outside the universe, outside space and time, where our Father is, and if we look at this mechanism from there, it appears completely different. What seemed to be necessity turns out to be obedience. Matter is total passivity, and consequently total obedience to the will of God. It is a perfect model for us. (*On Science, Necessity and the Love of God*, p. 178)[5]

(Here the "si nous transportons . . ." [if we transport] means that this account of material processes as something which is not blind necessity, but obedience, becomes something which cannot be discussed.) And I would not call it 'connaître' in the scientific sense of the word. From the point where we are, from our perspective, I can see no more ground for calling the tides and avalanches "obedience" than I would call a motor car obedient when it is being driven, or disobedient when it breaks down. One of the objections to speaking of 'obedience' as she does here is just that we do not know what disobedience would be. When the wind and the waves were said to obey Christ, they were *not* moving according to necessity or "obeying" natural laws. Even if I do not understand an order, I may do what was ordered by coincidence. But then it is not obedience. I do not obey the order unless I understand it. It is true that we speak of these and these natural happenings as obeying such and such laws of mechanics. But this is not like saying that they obey the *will* or *command* of anyone or anything. And it is no reason for loving them. Suppose nuclear fission obeys certain laws relating to mass and energy. But I do not see this as something to be admired. I do not admire the fidelity, reflecting that this is a situation in which I'd find fidelity difficult.

I do not understand this conception (or is it only a metaphor?) of physical laws as moral laws; as I should have to if I were to take "obedience" to them as a model for my own conduct, a model I should try to reach. As though any sort of regularity were to be admired and loved, were admirable just because it was regular. This is Kantianism with a vengeance.

Yet, I do not think this is a slip on Simone Weil's part, nor, in the ordinary sense, a confusion. She does want the analogy (or identity?) between physical laws and moral laws to be taken seriously. She would probably say that there is no real or fundamental distinction between them. And I have no doubt some will see what she means. It is connected, I think, with the notion of affliction—the pulverisation of the soul through matter and material suffering—as distance from God, and her idea of the point of great distance as the point which brings one nearest to God.

It is this kind of shift in her later writings that makes it hard to see where the discussion is going, what point is being made. Would she say that any genuine (véritable) understanding of mathematics must be understanding it from God's point of view? "God is always geometer." "Geometry is a theology."

Her conception of her own, or any human being's, obedience to the will of God is clearly important, but it is hard to grasp. One would have to grasp this, probably, before one could begin to understand what she means by "obedience" in physical things. This cannot mean that doctors should not stop a cholera epidemic; nor that nations should not try to stop Hitler's conquests.

It looks as though all obedience (or perfect obedience) to the love of God, and all true knowledge of *la réalité* would require complete *detachment*. *Intuitions Pré-Chrétiennes*, p. 157: "The contemplation of the reliability of things, whether it be in the visible world itself, in mathematical, or in analogous relations, is a powerful means of attaining it. The first lesson of this contemplation is not to choose, to give equal consent to all that there is. This universal consent is identical with detachment, and it seems that attachment, even the faintest or most legitimate, poses an obstacle to it."[6]

On the other hand, compare *L'Enracinement* p. 319: "The acquisition of knowledge causes us to approach truth when it is a question of knowledge about something we love, and not in any other case" (*The Need for Roots*, trans. A. F. Wills, London: Routledge and Kegan Paul, 1952, p. 242).[7] We might at first sight take this 'amour' for "attachment." But she speaks of an "amour de l'univers dans lequel nous vivons" (love of the universe in which we live), and it is not clear whether she would count this as attachment à un objet or not; but possibly not. *L'Enracinement* p. 329: "The spirit of truth can dwell in science on condition that the motive prompting the savant is the love of the object which forms the stuff of his investigations. The object is the universe in which we live. What can we find to love about it, if it isn't its beauty?" (*The Need for Roots*, p. 250).[8] Both these—to love the universe and (to love) the beauty of the universe—are phrases used in very special ways which deserve explanation.

Her first illustration of "l'amour d'un objet" in connection with "approcher de la vérité" had been the love of a man for a woman. When one speaks of a love of the universe in which we live, or a love of the beauty of the world, this seems a change of sense. For one thing, she would have said that this love of the beauty of the world was not an *attachment* in the sense in which the love of another human being may be. The example of man and woman is made clear through the *contrast* with what he learns of a woman he does not love. Her example contrasts what he learns about a woman he loves, and what he learns about some other woman of whom he has only just heard. I cannot contrast the universe in which I live with some other towards which I am indifferent. "But I can contrast that real world—reality—with what is imagined."

What marks her own personal obedience to the will of God in the action to be performed here and now? Granting that she has a love of the beauty of the world . . . what then? It would bring humility, kill self-assertiveness. But still there are decisions to be made; and perhaps one decision would show more perfect obedience to the will of God than another would. "Perfect passivity," waiting to be pushed, these clearly mean something, but only to those who have known what she did.

If we do emphasise the use of 'obey' in which the movements of a machine are said to obey the laws of mechanics, then we keep in mind that these are laws which hold in specific conditions; and also that it has been established by observation and experiment that these bodies (parts of the machine) so arranged do obey the laws of mechanics; or again that earthquakes and avalanches do. For other bodies, say fluids or gases in other circumstances, the behaviour would not be described as obedience to those laws, but to some others. Does the movement of a wave obey only those laws which the movement of a billiard ball does? The knowledge of the law is important just because it does have this special application. I do not know what it would mean to speak of some law which *everything* obeys, for which we cannot speak of the special circumstances in which it holds, the special sorts of events which are governed by it. Suppose that what Simone Weil calls "gravity" be action, movement, in accordance with some law which could be formulated. But then to say that all events or all developments obey the law of gravity would be empty and meaningless. If there is nothing which does not obey the law of gravity, then you are not describing what happens here and now when you say it obeys the law of gravity. It would be on all fours with: "whatever exists in a particular place at a particular time." In other words, the sense of 'obey' that is intelligible in connexion with mechanics has been lost.

"Everything happens in accordance with some mathematical necessity. So it follows that there is some mathematical necessity in accordance with which everything happens." (Adding perhaps that it is the contemplation of *this* [which?] necessity which is the precondition of seeing everything as obedience to the will of God. [?]) "Mathematical necessity" (in general) does not make *anything* necessary, does not make any conclusion necessary. Compare: "Everything happens in accordance with some plan. So there is some plan in accordance with which everything happens." Think of "We see purpose everywhere . . . so there is some grand purpose to which all we see is subordinate." And if we should add, "We must contemplate the necessity if we are to see everything as obedience to the will of God," I'd want to ask, "*Which*?"

Sometimes Weil speaks of 'la force', sometimes of 'les forces'. *Intuitions Pré-Chrétiennes*: "Despite the fact that he often vainly endeavours to maintain in himself the illusion to the contrary, man is here below the slave of natural forces that infinitely surpass him. This force that governs the world and makes all men obey, as a master armed with a whiplash does a slave, is identical with what the human mind understands by the term necessity."[9]

"Cette force"—suppose we asked which force is meant? Considering the acceleration of this body which we are observing, we can calculate or measure the force exerted by this body or that by these circumstances or those. But we do not measure the force exerted by (absolute) gravity. "The sun is a force affecting the movements of all the objects in the solar system. But gravity is a force affecting all movements everywhere and always."

I think she would want to *emphasise* that the notion of 'obedience' has a special sense in this connection (obedience to the will of God), although there are analogies with that of obedience of slave to master. There is something which would make it impossible to speak of servility here, for instance. But I do not know how explicitly this can be brought out. Perhaps only by means of analogies. And these may be illuminating to some, while others are not helped by them.[10]

On the other hand she seems to say that the necessity which illuminates the notion is the necessity which is recognised in *science*. The references to *rigour*, and so forth.

She calls mathematical necessity "conditional necessity," and she may be saying that there cannot be conditional necessity which does not rest on the "unconditioned." But I cannot see that she does say this. Consider: is there a parallel between (a) Obedience to the will of God is something different from obedience to the will of a man or an organization and (b) Self-discipline is something different from military discipline or discipline imposed by an organisation.

Compare 'l'ordre' in the sense of *logical* order, the order of a mathematical series or in a mathematical proof, with "Dans l'ordre du monde—dans l'ordre esthétique—quelle est cette chose?" (Simone Weil, *Connaissance*, p. 17). (What is this thing in the order of the world—in the aesthetic order?) "The order of the world" must be the order of a *theory* of the world. But this means nothing unless it means a general theory of physics. "L'ordre esthétique" would not be the idea of a general theory. This seems to be something like Kant's contrast between "the world of means" (cause and effect) and "the world of ends" ("Reich der Zwecke") leading on to critique of judgement (?). But then I am confused when she speaks of "the beauty of mathematics" side by side with the beauty of a stretch of mountain scenery.

As Weil sets out different conceptions of science, she also sets out different conceptions of necessity. The conception which she would find in classical mechanics is one which she had worked out, for instance, in her lectures, where she connected it with the understanding of the transformations of material things in terms of constructible models, that is, in terms of *mechanical* models, in terms of motions. And although she speaks of a "set of necessities," meaning by this, I suppose, a net of mechanical *laws* rather than a net of actual happenings (but this is not quite clear). In *Oppression and Liberty* she speaks of the whole of nature as a set of necessities, and this is confusing; still, this necessity is something that can be grasped only in the *activity* of the intellect (la pensée) in constructing models and working out the problems and reaching conclusions, and so forth. It is an activity of turning "constraint" into an "obstacle": it is an activity of analysing obstacles in accordance with a method (for understanding them), and in this way achieving what she later also calls a kind of equilibrium between the agent and the world. In all this, the necessity comes from us; it belongs to the method, to the order of operations in our thinking. And it is something which is, so to speak, introduced into the picture of the world that we construct. Only by the *application* of thought in action which follows a method. There is no method in the processes of nature themselves, no rule by which natural happenings proceed from the simple to the complex. The method, the intelligible order of the steps, comes from us.

It is the course of our construction that is important. And this is something which is changed in her later view. There is a change from the emphasis on activity and search and action (e.g. experimenting) to attention and contemplation. *Intuitions Pré-Chrétiennes*, p. 123: "L'âme de notre science est la démonstration. La méthode expérimentale en diffère du plus grossier empirisme que par le rôle qu'y joue la déduction" ("Descente," p. 123) (Demonstration is the heart of our science. The experimental method does not differ from the crudest empiricism, except for the role that deduction plays in it). I do not think this is true—see top of p. 124 especially: "D'après les documents actuellement en notre possession, il semble que les Grecs les premiers aient transporté la démonstration hors du domaine du nombre entier par l'invention de la géométrie et son application à l'étude de la nature" ("Descente," pp. 123–24). (According to documents currently in our possession, it seems that the early Greeks took demonstration outside of the domain of whole numbers by inventing geometry and applying it to the study of nature.)

One feature of her turning to Greek science was that she was turning less towards experiment. She says that the Greek scientists had given little attention to the application of their theories because they recognized that such applications may be used for good or for ill. Also:

> As for technical applications, if Greek science didn't produce many, it isn't because it was incapable of doing so, but because the Greek savants didn't wish it. These men, obviously very much less advanced than we are, as is natural seeing that they lived twenty-five centuries ago, feared the effects of technical inventions which could be made use of by tyrants and conquerors. So, instead of delivering to the public the greatest possible number of technical discoveries and selling them to the highest bidder, they kept rigor-

ously secret all the ones they happened to make for their own amusement; and, apparently, themselves remained poor. (*The Need for Roots*, p. 234)[11]

In any case it would seem more natural to speak of contemplation here (in connection with Greek science) than in connection with classical mechanics. Perhaps it was easier to think of necessity as geometrical necessity.

When Weil writes as though necessity were one thing, as though the word always meant the same, she is generally speaking of mechanical necessity, the necessary results of material forces or material conditions: the sinking of one arm of a balance when a weight is placed on it, or the breaking of a glass by a stone.

On the other hand, she had emphasised that when we observe the movement of a body or when we are studying, watching, a chemical reaction, this may be interrupted by some obstacle which we had not expected or reckoned with. When she speaks this way, she sees the difference between the outcome of material processes and the outcome or result of mathematical calculation or proof, where nothing emerges except what follows from the data contained and made explicit in the problem.

And yet Weil seems in other ways to be speaking as Wittgenstein did in the *Tractatus* when he said "there is only logical necessity" (no necessity other than logical necessity).

The necessity that we find in tracing the operation of a mechanical model is really the geometrical necessity in the steps of a construction. The operation of the model constructed follows from its structure. This necessity is something found only in the model, something that would belong to a closed system. And when we work from the conclusions which we reach through understanding the model or the construction to the predictions of actual occurrences, then there is something almost intelligible or miraculous in the fact that we are so often right or nearly right.

But otherwise Weil does not recognise physical impossibility as something different from mathematical or geometrical impossibility. At least this is so in much of what she says. There may be a difference *implied* when she is talking about physical processes. If she were *asked* what the necessity is there, she would say that this is a mathematical necessity, I suppose.

If we speak of forces operating, we are already introducing conceptions of measure; we are thinking of things in terms of mathematical relations between them.

This refusal to recognise different senses of the word 'necessity' is confusing, and not least when we consider the necessity of which she speaks in considering Greek science and her own idea of contemplation, as compared with the necessity recognized in Newtonian mechanics.

THE DISCIPLINE OF SCIENCE

Much of what Weil says about necessity, about the use of mathematics in the study of science, the study of what things are, how they are related to one another, much of this is an expression of something which could not be understood except by someone who had known the grace of God as she did. It needs not only religious faith, but a kind of religious insight, in order to understand the phrases or the figures or the grammar of what she writes.

This applies for instance to much of what she says about Greek science; about the views of Plato and the Pythagoreans. She makes observations about both which are illuminating, no matter what one's religious insight or lack of it. But she takes certain Pythagorean pronouncements apparently at their face value regarding the application of mathematics and the use of mathematics in describing material things. She speaks here in ways that invite criticism of the kind that one would give to ordinary philosophical discussions. Her views about mathematics and physics remind one also of Descartes, and they are put forward in a way which seems to take no account of the criticisms which Descartes's views met soon after his own writings appeared. She thinks of all matter as inert; and this reminds one of Descartes's treating of bodies as purely geometrical bodies. But this is also the Pythagorean view. It leads her to say that mathematics is the only true natural science.

Remarks of this kind invite academic criticism and seem wide open to it. But when I do try to criticise them in this way, I always suspect that I am being stupid, that I am failing (unable) to read what she has written in the way that it should be read, that I simply misunderstand something to which my eyes have not been opened. And then I conclude that I must leave it there.

She repeats, right to the end of her life, that science—and especially the discipline of science—is important in order to achieve a religious view of the world. She might say: the scientific view of the world and the religious view of the world are one and the same. This is because the scientific view of the world is the only one formed in accordance with stringent discipline, with attention to what she calls necessity. It is important to contemplate this necessity in order to free oneself from the illusions which spring up because we seek for features in the world which satisfy our personal desires. Contemplation of necessity coincides with "la contemplation parfaitment pure de la misère humaine" (the perfectly pure contemplation of human misfortune).

"The beauty of the world"—"The beauty of geometry"—"The beauty of mathematics."

"Nobody has ever tried to *sing* the calculus." Beethoven wrote on his *Missa Solemnis*: "Vom Herzen kommt es; mag es zum Herzen gehn" (it comes from the heart; may it return to the heart). Can one say this about a mathematical proof? As Weil *does* say it about natural beauty (e.g. page 133), "le rappel de cette double loi est ce qui nous atteint au coeur dans le spectacle du beau" (*La Science et Nous*), (it is because it reminds us of this double law that the spectacle of beauty pierces the heart, *Classical Science and After*, p. 12, where the scene is one resulting from "les nécessités aveugles de la matière" [the blind necessities of matter]).

Beethoven's setting for the *credo*.

Certainly one can find an aesthetic delight in the symmetry, the neatness or economy and the elegance of a mathematical proof. An impression of *perfection*. Everything falls into place and nothing is wasted. There is nothing *cumbersome* about it. And so forth.

But *beautiful*? Something which comes from the heart or goes to one's heart?

Simone Weil could see in mathematical (geometrical) ratios a representation of the Incarnation and of the role of Christ as Mediator. And it is clear that she does not think of this as a far-fetched representation. It is clear also that for her the conceptions of Christ and of the Incarnation were a deeper preoccupation and were more detached from personal ways of thinking than they have been for any but a few saints.

Her sense of the *distance* from God. Compare Prologue CS, p. 10, "Un jour il me dit: 'Maintenant va-t'en'" (*Connaissance*, p. 10). (One day he said to me: "Now go.") shows how much further her sense of God extended than does that of ordinary believers. And how entirely she kept her love of God a *pure* love: how freed (torn) from any sense of personal comfort, and her Prologue compare: "It is good for you that I go;

for if I do not go the Comforter will not come to you." Compare "L'amour est une chose divine. S'il entre dans un coeur humain, il le brise" (*Connaissance*, p. 294). (Love is something divine. When it enters the human heart, it breaks it). And how much deeper her devotion to the beauty and wonder of God is on this account.

À propos science *La Pesanteur et la Grace,* p. 170: "The privileged rôle of the intelligence in real love comes from the fact that it is inherent in the nature of intelligence to become obliterated through the very fact that it is exercised. (. . .) There is nothing nearer to true humility than the intelligence. It is impossible to be proud of our intelligence at the moment when we are not attached to it . . ." (Simone Weil, *Gravity and Grace*, London: Routledge and Kegan Paul, 1952, p. 116).[12]

All this hangs together with the attention which she gives to science. The discipline which keeps science from being anything personal, in that sense. But she would say that the same is true of the greatest art (Anonymity).

And this is connected with her treatment of geometry as an object of religious devotion (and not in any metaphorical sense). Love (devotion) is an "orientation"—attention, attente—not an emotion. This does not prevent her from speaking of *le coeur* (the heart) as what is visited by God. The "orientation" is an *orientation du coeur* (orientation of the heart).

Crucifixion, Passion . . . A deeper appreciation of the sense of tragedy among Greek philosophers and writers and in Greek religion, of the Greek attention to the suffering that goes with human existence, and their sense of and capacity for compassion.

If Weil were writing an academic discussion, if she were writing on the logic of science or of scientific method, then the remarks she makes (about necessity, for instance) would be open to a host of criticisms.

She speaks of the discipline which an artist observes in his work as the *same* discipline, or the same rigour as that of a mathematician or an experimental scientist. We are not inclined to challenge what she says here, but many would feel that this needs more explanation to show the possible ambiguities and to indicate how to avoid confusion as a result of them.

It would be possible to discuss and expound (or explain) details of her essay *La science et nous* (*Classical Science and After,* op. cit.)—her use of the expressions *images* and *imitation,* for instance.

But it is more important to try to grasp why Weil thought that an understanding of science, in the sense of understanding of what science is, than an understanding of the sense in which science may be said to provide or make possible "une connaissance du monde" (a knowledge of the world), why she thought this understanding was important or indispensable for the love of God.

"L'objet de la recherche ne doit pas être le surnaturel, mais le monde. Le surnaturel est la lumière; si on en fait un object, on l'abaisse." (The object of the inquiry must not be the supernatural, but the world. The supernatural is the light; if one turns it into an object, one debases it.) The point that "celui qu'il fait aimer est absent" (what we need to love is absent) and also: that God is not an object.

I must come to a clearer statement of the difficulty that her statement of her views does present; or what it is that I mean when I say that when I start to give an academic criticism of what she has said, I think I am being profoundly stupid.

She sometimes speaks almost as though Christ had been putting forward the same ideas as the Greek geometers. She sees in geometry what most of us do not and cannot see there, especially in the idea of arithmetic proportion. "What most of us do not and cannot see," although it may be that Pythagoras did. She is not thinking of a mean proportional as an abstract symbol which happens to present certain analogies, or just happens to be suitable as a symbol. She is taking it as involving an idea which *is* the idea of mediation between God and his creation or creatures.

It would be in a special way stupid to say that Pythagoras was making a *mistake* when he looked on geometry in that way. To us it seems strange, from various angles. If the understanding of geometrical theorems, and that means geometrical proofs, is a way of contemplating the divine mysteries (however this be understood), then prima facie it is strange to think that one can speak of 'correct' and 'incorrect'—of making a mistake in a proof, or of a difference between valid and invalid proof, and so forth. How does this fit in with the conception of *prayer*, for instance? And yet prayer, for Simone Weil, is *attention*, the same attention which goes to the contemplation of a theorem and its proof, such as that showing that every triangle inscribed in a semicircle is right angled.

The necessity of the conclusion of a geometrical proof is connected with the requirement of accuracy, stringency, exactitude. And Simone Weil suggests that the Pythagoreans would not have given that sort of attention to these things, would not have been so scrupulous in observing mathematical or geometrical exactitude, if they had not felt that it was a divine character (i.e., that the exact relations of, e.g., the sides of a right angled, or of an equilateral triangle, were or expressed some divine nature). But then it would seem as though the *necessity* of geometry, or more generally the necessity of mathematics, was divine. Perhaps the remark that the necessity holding in the material world is (or is seen as) a *conditional* necessity, would prevent this conclusion; I am not sure.

Prima facie there is a trouble here, because she wants to talk about the necessity of the created world, which is not divine. To trace this necessity is to show that divinity is *absent*. Perhaps this is the same as Plato's point when he remarks on the gulf between the necessary and the good, although in *Republic* 493 he is speaking of social affairs not of nature. This seems to be a persistent difficulty for my limited understanding of Weil's position: namely, that it is hard to see how she does distinguish mathematical necessity from the necessity of material happenings, what she calls "gravitation."

Perhaps something of the point is covered by what she says of "infinite error" and her speaking of material processes as "imitations" of mathematical concepts and operations. I imagine she had intended to go into the matter more fully, if she had finished the essay.

We might ask: Why does she find it "envirant" (exhilarating) to recognise that the truth of Christianity is expressed in the theorems of geometry? One reason may be because it brings out, or seems to illustrate so vividly, her conception of divine love as *lumière*. It is also, I suppose, because she thinks that the development of geometry by the Greeks was so much the work of genius (and this is admirable).

From the point of view of philosophy, it is interesting that the language of mathematics, or the grammar of mathematics, does have these tendencies, or that it can be seen in this way. That its importance can be found in this way.

There are two things here: the idea of mathematics as "a ritual," and again the idea of mathematics as showing something about the nature of the world. The Pythagoreans and Simone Weil would have said: showing the relation of the world to God.

Intuitions Pré-Chrétiennes, p. 124: "Il est merveilleux, il est inexprimablement envirant de penser que c'est l'amour et le désir du Christ qui a fait jaillir en Grèce l'invention de la démonstration" ("Descente," p. 124). (It is marvellous, it is inexpressibly exhilarating to think that it was the love and desire of Christ which gave rise to the invention of demonstration in Greece.)

Intuitions Pré-Chrétiennes, p. 163 infra: "Mais le Christ est la médiation même" ("Descente," p. 163). (But Christ is mediation itself.) p. 165: "Dieu est médiation, et toute médiation est Dieu" ("Descente," p. 165). (God is mediation, and all mediation is God.)

In these sentences we have religious utterances (figures, similes) which are not put forward for discussion. More plainly still, see *Intuitions Pré-Chrétiennes*, p. 37: "La beauté elle-même, c'est le Fils de Dieu. Car il est l'image du Père, et le beau est l'image du bien" ("Descente," p. 37). (Beauty itself, that's the Son of God. For he is the reflection of the Father, and the beautiful is the reflection of the good.)

In his connexion with *Philosophical Investigations* (when he was reading the early typescript version to me) there was a point when Wittgenstein spoke of an idea in the logic of language (or grammar of language)—I think it may have been connected with the notion of 'paradigms' (??)—where he said, "This is the same as what we have in the idea of a *Saviour*."

This is in some ways a remarkable parallel to Simone Weil's finding the idea of the Incarnation in the idea of proportion in geometry.

NOTES

Adapted from Notes dated 21.11.68;
18.11.68; 12.11.68; and 5.12.68.

1. "L'induction peut être considérée comme une application du principe: 'Les liaisons qui se répètent souvent peuvent être considérées comme constantes.' Dans l'induction, il y a un facteur purement mécanique, l'habitude, mais aussi on suppose que la constance est le signe de la nécessité. Puisque cette nécessité, nous ne l'avons pas constatée, amis supposée, nous sommes renvoyés à une élaboration d'hypothèses." *Leçons*, p. 100.

2. "L'ordre est quelque chose qui se déroule dans le temps, qui repose sur un rapport entre des opérations successives. Sans language, pas de souvenir: donc, une opération passée n'existerait plus." *Leçons*, p. 52.

Adapted from Notes dated 18.11.68;
21.11.68; 26.11.68; and 5.12.68 (Ed).

3. "Nous conférons aux choses et aux êtres autour de nous, entant qu'il est en nous, la plénitude de la réalité, quand à l'attention intellectuelle nous ajoutons cette attention encore supérieure qui est acceptation, consentement amour." *Leçons*, p. 155.

4. "Il y a analogie entre la fidélité du triangle rectangle à la relation qui lui interdit de sortir du cercle dont son hypoténuse est le diamètre et celle d'un homme qui, par example, s'abstient d'acquérir du pouvoir ou de l'argent au prix d'une fraude. La première peut être regardée comme un parfait modèle de la seconde." p. 156.

5. "La mécanisme de la nécessité se transpose à tous les niveaux en restant semblable à lui-même dans la matière brute, dans les plantes, dans les animaux, dans les peuples, dans les âmes. Regardé du point où nous sommes, selon notre perspective, il est tout à fait aveugle. Mais si nous transportons notre coeur hors de nous-mêmes, hors de l'univers, hors de l'espace et du temps, là où est notre Père, et si de là nous regardons ce mécanisme, il apparaît tout autre. Ce qui semblait nécessité devient obéissance. La matière est entière passivité, et par suite entière obéissance à la volonté de Dieu. Elle est pour nous un parfait modèle," *Pensées*, p. 97.

6. "La contemplation de la fidélité des choses, soit dans le monde visible lui-même, soit dans les relations mathématiques ou analogues, est un puissant moyen d'y parvenir. Le premier enseignement de cette contemplation est de ne pas choisir, de consentir également à l'existence de tout ce qui existe. Ce consentement universel est la même chose que le détachement, et l'attachement même le plus faible ou bien le plus légitime en apparence y fait obstacle." *Descente*, p. 157.

7. "L'acquisition des connaissances fait approcher de la verité quand il s'agit de la connaissance de ce qu'on aime, et en aucun autre cas." Simone Weil, *L'Enracinement*, Paris: Gallimard, 1949, p. 319.

8. "L'esprit de vérité peut résider dans la science à la condition que le mobile du savant soit l'amour de l'objet qui est la matière de son étude. Cet objet, c'est l'univers dans lequel nous vivons. Que peut-on aimer en lui, sinon sa beauté?" *Enracinement*, p. 329.

9. "L'Homme, bien qu'il s'efforce, mais souvent vainement, d'entretenir en lui-même l'illusion contraire, est ici-bas l'esclave des forces de la nature qui le dépassent infiniment. Cette force qui gouverne le monde et fait obéir tout homme, comme un maître armé d'un fouet fait obéir à coup sûr un esclave, cette force est la même chose que l'esprit humain conçoit sous le nom de nécessité." Simone Weil, *Descente*, p. 147.

10. Compare Wittgenstein's attitude to the use of Bunyan's allegory. See *Culture and Value*, pp. 28, 29, 77 (Ed).

11. "Quant aux applications techniques, si la science grecque n'en a pas beaucoup produit, ce n'est pas qu'elle n'en fût pas susceptible, c'est que les savants grecs ne le voulaient pas. Ces gens, visiblement très arrières relativement à nous, comme il convient à des hommes d'il y a vingt-cinq siècles, redoutaient l'effet d'inventions techniques susceptibles d'être mises en usage par les tyrans et

les conquérants. Ainsi, au lieu de livrer au public le plus grand nombre possible de découvertes techniques et de les vendre au plus offrant, ils conservaient rigoureusement secrètes celles qu'il leur arrivait de faire pour s'amuser; et vraisemblablement ils restaient pauvres." Simone Weil, *L'Enracinement*, p. 308.

Adapted from Notes dated 5.12.68;
9.12.68; 10.12.68; and 11.12.68 (Ed).

12. "Le rôle priviligié de l'intelligence dans le véritable amour vient de ce que la nature de l'intelligence consiste en ce qu'elle est une chose qui s'efface du fait même qu'elle s'exerce (. . .) Il n'y a rien de plus proche de la véritable humilité que l'intelligence. Il est impossible d'être fier de son intelligence au moment ou on l'exerce réellement. Et quand on l'exerce on n'y est pas attaché."

CHAPTER SEVEN

SCIENCE AND OBEDIENCE

HUMAN BEINGS AND THE WORLD

Simone Weil was interested in the relation of a human individual (any human individual) to the world. In her earlier work she had thought of this chiefly on Marxist lines: the ways in which the knowledge of natural processes, the kind of knowledge by natural science, enables human beings to make use of natural processes, and in this way to achieve a different kind of life from one that is tied incessantly to manual labour—to the securing of the material needs of existence. Social organisation and economic organisation have grown from the attempts to control the natural processes or conditions to which human beings are subject.

The relation of human beings to the world: she thought of this in her earlier work also on the lines of the Stoic love of the world expressed in the phrase *amor fati*.

If Marxists spoke of the relation of individual men to their material circumstances, they included in "material circumstances" their social circumstances, and here again Simone Weil would follow them. But she thought their account of oppression by "the social mechanism" was inadequate.

The relation of human beings to the world expressed in terms of physical labour: this conception she thought was Marx's principal contribution to western culture. The recognition of the need for a philosophy of labour. This conception of the philosophy of physical labour was one that she developed somewhat in terms of "notre pacte avec le monde" (our agreement with the world). In her later work she expressed this as the achievement of a kind of equilibrium between the human beings and the physical world. But it has to do, anyway, with the importance of the conception of *work* as developed in classical mechanics. And she saw the importance of classical mechanics chiefly in its interpretation of physical phenomena in terms of the conception of work (the product of force by distance) and the related conception of energy.

Her reference to Bacon's remark, that a man can command nature only in obeying it, interpreting this in terms of adapting oneself to circumstances by understanding them, or the possibility of adapting oneself which such understanding provides and the adapting oneself to "obstacles" through an understanding, analysis, of the obstacles. All this was made possible through the development of science. And in this way the development of science did give, or showed the way towards the possibility of the achievement of, some measure of freedom, overcoming exploitation.

Weil did not think, as the Marxists did, that this could be provided either through the increase of rationalising of social organisation—on the contrary; nor did she think that it would be the inevitable outcome of some dialectic of history.

So the relation of a man to the world is something that can be made clear, and so provide some sort of method by which a man may keep the course of his life in his own hands; he can do this in so far as his life consists of "action méthodique," and this is possible through the application and methods of science. That is the earlier view.

What this view left out was any adequate understanding and appreciation of good and evil in the world. Classical mechanics represented natural processes as indifferent to good and evil. Simone Weil thought this was true and salutary as far as our appreciation of our condition in the world is concerned. She spoke of classical mechanics as a "purification." And a part of what she meant was that the discipline and methods of physics help to free one from prejudice, that is, to avoid *imagining* that the world is so and so because such a world would satisfy our needs and desires. But when science is in the service of technology, it is *subservient* to particular ends, particular prejudices about what is important to discover. But it left, for instance, the conception of "our pact with the world" in a curious position, which one could express, to some extent, by asking: What is it that scientists are trying to do then?

Perhaps in her earlier work she would have answered in terms of *l'amour de la vérité*. But already in 1934 Weil saw some of the difficulties with this vague conception. The conception of mere accumulation of scientific discoveries or scientific facts, which did not seem to have any value and did not have any direct relation with clarifying thought. If our pact with the world is the understanding of the physical world, or even if we say that it is the achievement of some sort of equilibrium (however this is to be interpreted) between our own efforts and the fruits of them, well, what does it do for the life of the man who does achieve some sort of understanding in this way—for the life of a man whose life is guided by *action méthodique*? Might not such a life be evil? Or why is there any reason to think that there is such value in being guided by *la pensée* and by *méthode*?

The conception of 'l'amour de la vérité' did recognize something important in arriving at the understanding of the physical world (such understanding as physics had in some measure achieved); this value or importance is independent of the achievement of particular projects, independent of the practical side of it, in Marxist terms. (The difficulties about relativism and the idea of an absolute criterion of justice.)

One point was that an increase in our knowledge and mastery of natural processes was not making men (individuals) free. In a way it gives them less control over their lives and less understanding of them than would be possible under more primitive conditions. And it does not give them understanding in their lives, does not give them understanding of their relation to the world. And this is the conception that is important to her.

To ask about the relation of human beings to the world, or *a* human being in the world in which he is, is to ask something about the value of the world; or the value of the sort of reality that is presented by the scientific account. The relation of this to value. Weil thought that Greek science had tried to take account of this, to show something about the value of the world, giving an account which showed the beauty (or order) of the world.

If we speak of a man's relation to necessity, this can be given only to a very minor extent by Bacon's maxim. This leaves out of account the ways in which human beings are crushed by the forces they understand. Although this point should have been obvious in the conception of the indifference of physical laws to good and evil.

This meant, I suppose, that the relation of a man to the world could not become clear except through the love of God; except in so far as he appreciated the beauty of the world. What then is the relation between what becomes clear through the love of God and what becomes clear through science?

To have a love of God and to have an understanding of one's relation to the world are one and the same thing. So one may have an understanding of one's relation to the world without an understanding of science. As most of the great religious teachers and mystics showed.

The idea that knowing the physical laws by which one's actions are governed—knowing the necessities to which one is subject—was the best guide to obedience to the will of God (the view is like Spinoza's) seems to have more connexion with the rest of her religious ideas.

On the other hand, it is hard to see that she herself did rely much on this. This would be no refutation. But it is hard to find examples of the sort of "submission to necessity" which she seems to speak of.

Weil thought that science was a system of general laws, and in her later view she thought it was reducible to mathematics. She thought of the supernatural and of the grace of God in terms of the operation of general laws as well. I do not know that she ever gave any reason for this. At least, I do not see her reasons for insisting that the working of 'the supernatural' was the working of "a mechanism" unless this be assumed. Although I can see the idea of divine love or of *le surnaturelle* as *une lumière*, and that one degrades it if one looks on it as a *consolation*. The importance of her insistence that God is not an *object*.

METHODICAL OPERATION

Simone Weil suggests that the operation with signs in higher algebra is often "blind" in the sense that one does not know what the signs signify; and that sometimes one does not understand what the operation has to do with the result which is reached, as when a certain combination of e and i in combination with 'pi' can be operated so as to show the impossibility of the quadrature of the circle. She contrasts such work with what she calls "la pensée méthodique." She contrasts a methodical operation, for which insight into the meanings of the signs, and perhaps into the sense of the operations would be required (as when one understands division by seeing its relation with multiplication), with an application in accordance with or in conformity with a method, since this may be practised without any understanding of the method or of why it is used in this particular case.

It is surely wrong to say that "an entirely free life would be one in which the only real difficulties one encountered would be of the sort which we meet in the problems of geometry and arithmetic, and in which overcoming a difficulty was like working out a solution in action."[2]

In mathematics we always know what a solution would be like; we always know the form that a solution would have. In this sense we always know the end which we are trying to achieve. But when people have to decide what course to take in their lives, it is generally not like this. As, in some measure, Weil recognizes.

Later, when she is contrasting la personne et le sacré, she speaks of mathematical activity as *anonyme*; and, if I remember, she speaks of the work of a manual labourer, when he is guided simply by his understanding of necessity—when he is pursuing the job as he does because of his understanding of it—then this is *anonyme* in the same way.

In both cases she seems to be taking the solution of a geometrical or an engineering problem as the paradigm of coming to a decision. In what she would call the ideal case of free action there would be nothing to decide: it is only a question of "la pensée méthodique" in connexion with "éléments donnés."

If you can see *why* you do what you do, if your action follows from your own judgment of the éléments donnés, then you are free.

This is her account of *pure* activity or pure decision, in the sense in which geometry is pure, and as impossible in the real world as the objects of geometry are.

"On ne peut rien concevoir de plus grand pour l'homme qu'un sort qui le mette directement aux prises avec la nécessité nue, sans qu'il ait rien à attendre que de soi, et tel sa vie soit une perpetuelle création de lui-même par lui-même."[3] (N.b.: ". . . sans qu'il ait rien à attendre que de soi"—without his being able to expect anything except through his own exertion.) Later she speaks of this same sort of thing as *anonyme*.

I agree that in many—perhaps most—free activities, what is important about the work accomplished is not that it has been performed by me. This is true of the solution of a mathematical problem, for instance. And it is true—whether in just the same sense or not—of artistic work. What she says about the anonymity of this is important.

But "creating the material conditions of one's own life" is something different. It is something which I must do, and it will not do to imagine it anonymous.

Still more so where we are considering my relations to other people. There are difficulties enough here, whether one wishes to call them problems or not. And it will not do to say that if a solution of these difficulties is reached, then it need not be thought of as having a special relation to me, as though it made no difference whether I were responsible for it or someone else was. Consider the deep problems of marriage, for instance: it is essential that if either one of the partners offers something towards a solution, then it must come from him, since it is addressed to the other partner, and what is important is that he should be doing something. (Simone Weil is pretty oblivious to this kind of difficulty.)

Although the greatness of *Lear* might be called "anonymous," it would be senseless to say that the play had been produced from éléments donnés through la pensée méthodique. The work was free in the sense that it was not carried out according to directions received from elsewhere. But it would probably be wrong to speak of it as a work of la pensée, in the sense in which she is speaking of this.

For Weil, the relation of thought to the work of completing the solution of the mathematical problem presents no difficulty. Perhaps we could call this an internal relation. At any rate, there is nothing which we might call the thought *plus* the solution of the problem.

If we could construct a machine so that the steps of its operation were like the steps in the solution of a mathematical problem, then the relation of thought to this physical operation would not present any difficulties either. It would be like a problem in pure mechanics, perhaps.

But she sees a difficulty in the relation of thought to the movements of my own body. "Une ombre impénétrable enveloppera toujours le rapport immédiat qui lie nos pensées à nos mouvements."[4]

I think this is a misconception of the problem about the relation of thought and action, and especially of the relation of decision and action. (She seems hardly to see two different questions here.)

Her trouble is that we cannot treat our bodily movements as presenting us with problems in pure mathematics. (Perhaps if we could, we should be able to control the body with no trouble.) As though the bodily actions would be intelligible if bodily operations *were* mental operations, or if thought could *penetrate* the actions and have insight into their necessity. As if the body were a perfectly constructed machine which the mind could operate. How does this affect what has to be *decided*, though?

Thinking of the relation of thought and bodily movement as the attempt to carry out an *application* of thought to something which cannot be well understood, whereas the application of my thought to a problem in mechanics can be quite clear. If only my body were a machine!

Think of the relation between an order and carrying out an order. This may illustrate the relation of thought and action of a kind, but it does not carry it very far. And her way of treating the problem leaves out the 'I', so that it does not touch what seems to me the most important and the most difficult problem.

Her example of a pilot guiding a ship. (If this is meant to illustrate the relation of will and action—or will and the body it controls—then I think the example is uncommonly poor.) Knowing what to do would be knowing what factors are involved, and knowing what would have to be done in order to guide one's reactions to them. What is needed in order to escape destruction, or in order to meet certain obstacles, and so on.

Contrast Kierkegaard's discussion in *Der Begriff der Angst* (*The Concept of Anxiety*). Her treatment of 'le vide' seems to be connected with this. Giving up wishes which are seen to be vain, for instance.

But if Weil thinks that the only reasons which influence action—or which ought to influence action—are those from a consideration of necessity, of what it is possible to do and what it is not possible to do, then I should say that she was misconceiving the nature of necessity and of pure love. The purity would consist in being guided not at all by one's passions, and only by the recognition of what is the only path allowed by necessity. Love has no sense at all, it is a form of slavery to the passions, except in so far as it is a form of love of the world or of necessity.

Contrast this notion of purity with that of Kierkegaard in *Purity of Heart*.

For Simone Weil love of necessity would be the same as the love of God—perhaps because it is pure obedience. The main point seems to be that one's actions are not influenced by anything which is arbitrary—anything which comes from the imagination. Doing what has to be done—what is the only thing to do—regardless of what one may wish or desire. (But I still am not clear just what she does understand by pure necessity. And neither am I sure what she might mean by making or building the material conditions of one's existence, especially if this is not supposed to include the satisfaction of any desire. Perhaps the point would be in some sort of distinction between rational and irrational desires.) We need examples of situations in which one might say, "There was nothing else I could do." What is strange is her wish that they might *all* be like this (p. 117: ". . . sans qu'il ait rien à attendre que de soi . . . par lui-même"—without his being able to expect anything except through his own exertion).

Here 'de soi' means 'de sa pensée'. And she seems almost to define thought or thinking by reference to the solution of mathematical problems.

But in solving a mathematical problem I may appeal to someone else for help, or I may ask him to confirm or check what I have done. "Have I got this right?" And the same would apply to problems in engineering.

Certainly you may say that I cannot perform a calculation or solve a problem or draw a logical conclusion unless I myself can see that this conclusion follows.

But ex hypothesi I am not *responsible* for the conclusion. And for this reason 'I' do not enter into it—it is not like coming to a decision or doing what I have decided to do. For when I am coming to a decision (or trying to) this is *not* a performance that another could have done (as though someone might have told me or pointed out to me what the conclusion is). The solution of the mathematical problem is not "mine" in the sense in which my action is. (Apart from actions of this kind, I should hardly have any "idea of myself" at all.)

What makes the action mine is not that I have insight into the necessity of the conclusion. There need be nothing *at all* like that. Nor is the decision mine simply because I depend upon my own judgment (perhaps about what ought to be done). For I may depend only upon my own judgment when I am criticising someone else. 'Judgment' in what sense? She does not make the distinction clear, and her example of mathematics is misleading.

There is perhaps a difficulty in saying what decisions are—just from the fact that they may be made for certain reasons or at any rate may be discussed in terms of reasons for and against them. For I have suggested that if it were not that the decision were accessible to reasons, the 'I' would not enter into it. And if coming to a decision were simply carrying out a piece of reasoning, then I could have learned the conclusion from someone else. (Cf. Kant's conception of the rational will: actions which follow from principles.)

Aristotle and the practical syllogism. I expect Plato would have called this sophistry. "The art of reaching the true conclusion; the art of finding the right answer." This appears as sophistry especially in connexion with politics. The *Gorgias* on sophistry as the counterfeit of legislation, which is understood there as the art of making people better, apparently.

Contrast Socrates's method of catharsis, which may be what Simone Weil thinks she is describing.

Self-confrontation. Seeing the difference between what is genuine and what is illusion or counterfeit, between a life which is awake and a life which is a lie. There seems to be nothing of this in Aristotle.

Certainly there can be no formal account of how such decisions are made (the sort of decision with which Alcibiades was faced). And the practical syllogism could tell one little about it.

Small wonder that Aristotle saw the chief difficulty in the form of *weakness* of will. Anybody can see what the right conclusion *is*; the difficulty is in carrying it out.

But even if we described the plight of Alcibiades as one of weakness of will, it would not be a question of making practical a conclusion from general principles.

"The mechanism of decision." The idea of a *method* for deciding, or for solving practical problems. (Vide Stocks's criticism of Aristotle in his essay on the golden mean.[5] The neglect of questions of self-sacrifice, for instance. And, incidentally, the decision with which Alcibiades was faced seems to have little or nothing to do with finding a mean, whatever part this may play in the table of goods in the *Philebus*.)

The application of a method. The notion of intelligence in practical affairs, as conceived, for instance, by the utilitarians.

"Can virtue be taught?"

Is the practical syllogism meant as something like the introduction of a calculus into practical affairs? If it were, would it be comparable to the 'calculus' of the utilitarians?

The philistine notion that ethics has to do with the search for a measure of our likes and dislikes. And the still more philistine notion that this measure is to be found in pleasure.

What is important is the sense of good and evil, not the fact that people have different likes and dislikes (with the "problem" of how these likes and dislikes are to be reconciled). Bentham apparently at a loss to find some standard for criticism of likes and dislikes: his objection to all previous standards as "arbitrary."

If there were such a "method of solving practical problems," then convincing you of a mistake in your decision would be like showing you a mistake in your calculation.

When Socrates speaks of making a mistake in what you choose or what you prefer, he means something entirely different from this. It is not a matter of miscalculating what the results are going to be. And there is an important sense in which the person himself is the only one who can discover his mistake. The importance of 'self-confrontation' is connected with this. So is the reference to his method as 'catharsis'. And especially the recognition of the difference between genuine and sham: we might almost say that the whole of the *Republic* is concerned with this. But there is no suggestion of any principle or formal method which will enable you to recognise this. (Plato was preoccupied with it for the rest of his life. The *Sophistes* is meant to give an account of it—at least of the distinction between genuine discourse and sham discourse. But I do not think he was pretending to give any formal answer.)

The sense of what is degrading, or the sense of good and evil. It is this which Socrates awakened in men. Whereas the practical syllogism always takes it for granted—something you can discover by reflecting on the practices of the best people.

Compare the idea of 'moral instruction', perhaps as understood by the church.

The absurdity of "a machine that decides." (Think of the way 'I' enter into my actions.)

We may think of a machine which solves problems in construction or calculation: it solves the kind of problems which can be solved by calculation.

But in making decisions we are often faced with problems of a different sort. No sort of calculation could have helped Alcibiades.

NOTES

Adapted from Notes dated 25.1.69; and 5.6.69.

1. From undated notes (Ed).

2. Simone Weil, *Oppression and Liberty*, p. 86.

3. Simone Weil, "Réflexions sur les Causes de la Liberté et de l'Oppression," in *Oppression et Liberté*, Paris: Gallimard, 1955, p. 117. Trans: "It is not possible to conceive of a nobler destiny for man than that which brings him directly to grips with naked necessity, without his being able to expect anything except through his own exertion, and such that his life is a continual creation of himself by himself." Simone Weil, *Oppression and Liberty*, p. 87.

4. Ibid., p. 120. Trans: "The immediate relationship linking our thoughts to our movements will always remain wrapped in impenetrable obscurity." Simone Weil, *Oppression and Liberty*, p. 89.

5. "The Golden Mean," in J. L. Stocks, *Morality and Purpose*, edited by D. Z. Phillips, London: Routledge, 1969.

CHAPTER EIGHT

SCIENCE OR RELIGIOUS MEDITATION?

Her 1933–1934 lectures and her earlier writings on social theory do belong to what I am calling 'academic philosophy'. And in much of what she says after 1939 Simone Weil seems to write as though there were a continuity, as though she were simply going further, perhaps deeper, in the lines in which she had been working before. It is because she seems to pass from the one way of speaking to the other so easily, as though it were no occasion for comment, that it is so hard to criticise, or for that matter to expound or paraphrase what she is saying.

Weil thinks, apparently, that questions expressed in religious meditation or in remarks concerning moral judgements or difficulties have some important connections with questions in the philosophy of science: questions regarding the application of mathematics and of physical theories, the relation between ideal constructions and the natural processes or obstacles we run against. If there are serious confusions here, I think there is much (including those confusions) which is worth discussing.

If we only had a considerable part of what is in *Gravity and Grace* I'd feel that this was a real and profound philosopher. But then I should be imagining, in a very general way, the kind of thinking from which (I'd suppose) these fragments came. And that is not what I find when I study what she did write *about science* in the last three or four years of her life. Her lectures at Roanne, 1933–1934,[1] were certainly philosophy. And although I may not go along with everything she says in them, I feel I know where I am. This is so especially of what she said in those lectures about the philosophy of science (about science as a form of knowledge). I do not think she was a great philosopher, but her lectures show that she was a talented one. She might have become a very good philosopher if she had devoted herself to it. With her writings from 1940 to 1943 it is different. If I think I have come upon something that is inadequate or confused or that is a fault in her Roanne lectures, I think I have learned something in becoming aware of this. But however much I study her later writings on *science*, I do not think I have learned anything at all. I am inclined to say that what she wrote then is not philosophy but religious meditation. This would not be anything against it, and my remark would not be meant as derogatory. Almost all her time was devoted, with extraordinary concentration, to these things. She was an important writer on political philosophy. But her greatness lay in her meditations on moral and religious questions. And I doubt if 'greatness' is the word to use here. I think of her as a saint. This shows in her life, as far as I know of it. And it shows in her *Notebooks* (including *La Connaissance Surnaturelle*, Paris: Gallimard, 1950) and in certain of her letters and essays. Most of her later writings were partly religious meditation. This is true even of *L'Enracinement* (Paris: Gallimard, 1949).[2] And it is true of her essays on science. It is this which makes it particularly hard to know how to read or criticise various things she says.

I do not think one can say simply that her discussions ought to be purged of those remarks which seem to belong to religious contemplation. For if we tried to do this, then what was left would not be at all the discussion she is giving. But I agree there are *difficulties* in seeing one's way through this.

If it were just that Simone Weil wrote in religious meditation and not in philosophy, I should have no complaint. But I feel like complaining that she *mixes up* philosophy and religious meditation, and writes as if she were not even aware that she was doing so. She would tell me this shows how little I understand, and I am sure she would be right. And no doubt I should leave it there: I do not understand. Full stop. But can someone tell me the address of someone who *does* understand so that I might ask him *how* I ought to look at her writings?

If we consider the main point or sense of what she writes in the long (but unfinished) essay *La Science et Nous*,[3] for instance, we recognize that this is not a discussion of the logic of science, that it is not concerned with the difference between calculation and experiment, with what a scientific problem is, with the different roles of hypotheses and the different forms of confirmation in science, with what is meant by discovery, and so on, as, *nota bene*, she *had* been when she spoke of science and the other forms of knowledge in *Leçons de Philosophie*. I repeat: the philosophy of science in this sense is not her theme or concern in these later essays. And for this reason it is very foolish to start with questions and criticisms which would be appropriate to a philosophical discussion. Perhaps this would be stupid in somewhat the way in which Frazer was stupid in reading the rites and religious practices of other cultures as crude attempts to do what western scientists really know how to do.

She is trying to speak of science in the language that belongs to religious meditation. In the essay "Descente de Dieu" in *Intuitions Pré-Chrétiennes* (Paris: La Colombe, 1951, pp. 9–172), which is a much more finished essay than the set of notes "God in Plato," she speaks of seeing all natural happenings and relations among natural things as forms of necessity, and she means there *mathematical* necessity. And she says this is a higher step than recognising simply that everything in nature is governed by "force," but that it is still not viewing material processes as examples of perfect *obedience* to the will of God, and that *this* step is not one for which there is any method: it is not a step which a human being himself can take, unless he is led to it by the reception of divine grace. In other words, none can know what she is speaking of, what she does understand by 'obedience' unless he has known the Grace of God as she has. Obviously I would raise no objection to her saying this—or none to such a statement on its own account. The difficulty is that she does not seem to intend *everything* she says to be intelligible only to those whose hearts are with God as hers is.

Further, in some passages Weil *is* writing the philosophy of science. But she does this, for example, in order to show why she is justified in *discarding* some of the work of scientists. This is what she is doing in her discussions of quantum mechanics, I think. I would call these discussions 'the philosophy of science', although she would have modified them had she lived longer. I would guess that she has a case in some of what she says. But I think also that she misunderstands some of the principal points which she attacks. But I do not think this matters very much. She wants to show that quantum mechanics is not "une science véritable" (a true science), and here again we are at a point where I am uncertain whether to criticise or not. In secular language, I think such a phrase as "une science véritable" (where it is not a matter of distinguishing science from pseudo-science) shows confused metaphysics. And I want to counter with one of Wittgenstein's remarks: "Science is what scientists do." It cannot be the work of philosophy to say what "real science" would be. On the other hand, she may now be speaking in the language which sees a chemical reaction as an example of perfect obedience which can serve us as a model in our own lives. And then I must be still.

When she writes about mathematical and physical necessity in "La science et nous," for example, she says that the true physics is found in mathematics. And since the results of physical measurements and the observable happenings that are predicted are always "plus or minus," she speaks of "an infinite *error*" involved when we use mathematical formulae in our descriptions of natural happenings; and she thinks it is an inexplicable mystery that what is calculated in mathematical physics does so often lead us to predictions that are confirmed. From everything she says here, it would appear that she had not begun to ask herself how mathematics *is* used in physics, or to distinguish between the use of mathematical propositions in calculation and the use of empirical laws in description: the true *description* would be what is given in pure mathematics. Once more, her lectures at Roanne[4] show us that she was alive to these questions, or many of them. And so I am entirely foxed as to what she *is* trying to do in that later essay.

Very often when she refers to Plato, this only confuses matters further. For one thing, in the *Timaeus* and in the *Republic* too, Plato *contrasts* 'necessity' and 'reason' (*nous*, to which he would give all mathematics). Simone Weil says repeatedly that Plato emphasised the gulf that divides "nécessité" and "le bien" ('necessity' and 'the good'). But she also writes as though seeing mathematical necessity in the whole of nature were a precondition to an understanding of that perfect obedience to the will of God which should be a paradigm to human efforts.

But here I must be more careful, for she probably means this in the Pythagorean or Platonic sense of 'imitation'. In *Intuitions Pré-Chrétiennes* she adopts a Pythagorean view of mathematics, according to which pure mathematics is simultaneously a formal calculus and discipline, a theory of nature and of natural happenings, and a religious mystical doctrine. But I have *no* idea what it means, and I have just to back away and sit down. I do not know *what* Pythagoras recognised when he celebrated his geometrical discovery about triangles inscribed in a semi-circle with a religious feast. It is interesting and gratifying that she herself finds the conception of 'imitation' as the most obscure and the most in need of clarification of the concepts she uses in her account of Greek science in *La Science et Nous.*[5]

The *Timaeus* suggests that if someone contemplates the regular movements of the heavenly bodies, contemplates them in the study of astronomy, which Plato seems to have treated rather as pure hermeneutics, and a branch of pure mathematics, this contemplation will help to bring regularity into the movements of the soul of the student through imitation. I guess Simone Weil had this in mind. On the other hand, I do not think there is much about the *will* of God in the *Timaeus*.

In the *Republic* it is said that the sensible world is the offspring of the intelligible world, or that it stands to the intelligible world in the relation of image (shadow, reflection in water) to what casts the image. In other words, the sensible world *depends* on the intelligible world, in some way, but we understand this only in terms of analogy. But not only is the sensible world dependent, it seems to be *derived* from the intelligible world in some way (offspring, *ékegonos*), and in this sense "determined by it." The perfect model of this derivation would be a calculation and the result it yields. But the dependence of the sensible world is an imperfect imitation of this. (What of *perfect obedience?*)

Now this is unsatisfactory or unintelligible to us, in so far as it suggests that material processes (movements of the tides, chemical reactions) are *derived from* the mathematical expressions we use in describing them. However, for this account of Plato's, some analogy to it might be elaborated, the relations between physical necessity and mathematical necessity are just as obscure as ever. For in such an account there is no discussion of what causal laws are and how they are established (how would you establish any empirical law in biochemistry, for instance?). There is hardly any reference to empirical regularities, regular sequences. In fact, the only reference that comes to my mind is in the account of the "games" which prisoners in the Cave play with the successions of shadows they watch (*Republic* VII). And Plato is suggesting that this—drawing conclusions from observed regularities—has nothing to do with genuine science. Yet when Simone Weil speaks of the "perfect obedience" with which material forces follow the will of God, she is speaking of perfect regularities, and these are regularities which can be found by observation, measurement, experimental methods and statistics, they are *empirical* regularities. You see how easily I can find myself back at square one.

When we have been reading what she writes about science, the big question is always: what does this show regarding the love of God?

She criticises Pascal's view, expressed in the way he imagines God speaking to his creatures: Tu ne me chercherais pas, si tu ne me possédais;

ne t'imaginête donc pas.[6] All that she says about the mistake of *searching* for God is connected with this. She would say, I imagine, that that expression of Pascal's would leave the road wide open to idolatry. (God is that which would satisfy a man's—*any* man's?—deepest longings. More vulgarly still, God is the object of the heart's desire. And together with this: the world is ordered for the good of man: everything in the world is there for the use of man, etc.) The study of science, if you study science seriously, is a corrective to this. You cannot any longer look on the world as ordered for the benefit of men.

The mistaking of God's love for something like consolation or comfort. "L'amour n'est pas consolation, il est lumière."[7] If she says that God enters in and fills "le vide,"[8] this is entirely different from saying that God satisfies a longing. This is part of what she means when she says that the study of science may be a *purification*, a purification from idolatry.

The methods of science, the methods of scientific criticism, are important in science—in *physics* (for that is what she generally means). This is the way men must go if they want to rid their minds of false beliefs in physics. But I do not know any passage in which she makes it plausible to think that these methods will guide one in ridding one's mind of false ideas in religion. And *nota bene*, she would not admit what I should think obvious, that it is a different sense of 'false' (just *because* there is a different meaning to "showing that it is false") in the one case and in the other.

But then we have to remember that the more complete or true methods of science would be designed to show the beauty of the world, as, Weil would contend, Greek science was. Perhaps she would say that the beauty of the world cannot be shown in any other way (I am not sure). And here again I think she is giving expression to a religious insight which I cannot hope to understand. It is not just that she had not worked out her account of Greek science as she had intended to do. It is that she speaks of "beauty" here in a way which I suspect must mean nothing to those without religion. She speaks of the "beauty" of mathematical proofs, of the beauty of a natural science, of the beauty of a dramatic tragedy, of the beauty of a piece of music—as though anyone could see that one means the same in each case. I'd have said it was obvious that one might recognise the beauty of a tragedy, and yet not know what is meant by speaking of the "beauty" of mathematics, even when one understands it. If Beethoven wrote on the manuscript of his *Missa*

Solemnis, "Vom Herzen kommt es, mag es zum Herzen gehn" (It comes from the heart, may it go to the heart), nothing of this sort would be said by the general run of people who find delight in mathematics. (Pythagoras was different.) More important, I do not understand her phrases when she speaks of "the beauty of the *world*" or "the order of the world." Sometimes it seems as though she were speaking of the uniformity of nature. But this would give nothing like the unity of a beautiful object. Indeed, in other connections, I'd have thought she would not want to speak of *the world* as an object at all.

Weil writes as though the result is to be *expected* from the study of science, as if we could assume that it would have this result in most people. Whereas, as I think she recognises, in other connections the study of science may make men absurdly arrogant, "we can be masters of our destiny, we can assume the role of God," or make them devoted to technology and thence to prestige and power. I would guess that only very few scientists know of the purification of which Simone Weil is speaking. The easy answer might be, "Well, the study of science may be *necessary* for purity in the love of God, although it is not *sufficient*." But she would not say this. I do not suppose Buddha or Jesus or St. Paul had studied science.

I think that for Simone Weil the intimate connection of science and religion went with her idea that the truth of religion is independent of any historical tradition, like that of the Hebrews. It went with (her idea of) a *universality* of religion—the same spirit finding its expression in different religious forms in different localities, different folklore and practices, and so on.

But in the first place, if we speak of the generality of Christian ideas, for instance, saying perhaps that they are true for all men, this is not at all like the "universal validity" of mathematics. When she spoke of the love of God, she would include other forms of worship than Christianity. But this makes the difference still more pronounced.

The point I would emphasise here: that all the mathematical scientific methods, whether of Greek science or classical mechanics, leave you with a certain relativity. Scientific problems (of physics or biology) and possible answers to them have meaning *within a system*—in relation to a method of investigation, of proof and disproof, testing and confirmation, and in relation to a notation. When Simone Weil speaks of "une véritable science" (almost like "what investigation would be, if it were *really* investigation") she confuses this. But if she suggests that a genuine science, perhaps Greek science, would show the world as God sees it, this cannot be something which she learned from science or from contemplating science. It must rest on the religious conviction which she has independently of any science.

But if science has the sort of relativity I have mentioned, this must affect the sense in which it purges religion of idolatry. And if we do speak of 'purification' in her sense, then I suppose we will feel compelled to speak of "une véritable science."

The difficulty with speaking of 'purification' in this way is that it suggests a kind of *absolutism*. It reminds me of the idea of 'complete analysis' in Wittgenstein's early logic.

On the other hand, in view of the prestige of science in our culture, and the way in which this has affected the thinking of almost everyone (or rather of *everyone*, without qualification) it may be said that you cannot speak in a religious way about the world or about human life unless you do consider how science speaks. Well, granting this, I can only say that I cannot make out what she is saying in this field. This is because I do not know how the whole thing looks from the standpoint of the love of God—the standpoint from which she is writing.

All this is just to say that I cannot follow her remarks on science and the love of God. And this is all I have shown.

Kierkegaard has one great advantage: that he does not feel he must write about science as she does. I would generally say that her religious observations go deeper than Kierkegaard's.

I have understood from her writings what is meant by thanks to God for a realisation that one's own existence has no worth, and in this connection, what it means to speak of feeling *equal* gratitude for joy and for affliction.

I have not found this understanding in any other religious writer— St. Paul, St. Augustine, or Kierkegaard, for instance.

On a very great number of questions I have found remarks of hers which are more illuminating than any others I know. That is often so on "secular" matters, as in connection with the Pythagorean discovery of the incommensurability of the diagonal and the side of a square, for instance. She is an example of a writer whose greatness of soul comes out in frequent remarks, which makes the difficulties or shortcomings of her more theoretical observations seem of no importance at all.

Remarks in which she shows a soul or character before which I can only stand still, which I could no more imagine than I could have imagined Bruckner's music if I had not heard it. Something like gratitude (it would be stupid to speak of admiration).

In her later writings, during 1940–1943, she wrote of submitting to the necessity shown by the natural sciences:

> The mechanism of necessity can be transposed on to any level and remain the same. It is the same in the world of inert matter, in plants, in animals, in nations, and in the souls of men. Seen from where we are, in our perspective, it is an entirely blind mechanism. But for anyone whose heart goes out beyond himself, beyond the universe, beyond space and time, to where our Father is, and regards this mechanism from there, it looks entirely different. What seemed to be necessity becomes obedience. Matter is complete passivity, and so complete obedience to the will of God. For it is a perfect model. In a view of its perfect obedience, matter deserves to be loved by those who love its Master . . .[9]

When she says that material processes show not blind necessity but obedience, only those whose hearts have been with God can follow her.

"Men can never evade obedience to God. A creature cannot *not* obey. The only choice open to a man as an intelligent and free creature, is to desire to show obedience or not to desire it. . . . If he desires it, he is still subject to mechanical necessity, but a new necessity is added to (superimposed on) it, a necessity from the laws belonging to what is through him, sometimes almost in spite of him."[10]

Simone Weil writes as though we ought to take the regularity of the tides, of the fall of unsupported bodies, as models of perfect obedience to the will of God. To look on necessity—the operation of natural forces—as something to be loved, is the same as *consenting* to necessity. "This consent is a form of foolishness (folie), a foolishness proper to men. . . . The love that St. John bore for him who was his friend and his lord, while he was leaning on his breast during the Last Supper, this is the love we ought to bear for the mathematical chain of causes and effects which, from time to time, reduces us to a formless pulp. Obviously this is mad" (*Intuitions Pré-Chrétiennes*, pp. 148–50).[11]

"Manifestement cela est fou." She is not trying to persuade people of the *reasonableness* of such consent. Not even of what is meant by it. She says only that when someone shows it, he has shown the love of God to the full.

She speaks of the necessity of actual processes—what goes on in the laboratory, the fall of the rock that crushes me—as an "imitation" of the necessity expressed in a mathematical demonstration. Here again, I do not think she has blundered. But I do not know what she is saying.

Every creature, she says, is subject to the necessity of time. And here the physical necessity expressed in classical mechanics can be seen as that which we also know as oppression in the lives of human beings. Most of the problems in anyone's life are centred round his relations to what is past, to what it is not yet (the relation between a desire, or a deed, and its accomplishment), or to duration (the break-up of a person through the length of his suffering or his servitude). We might say a man is free when time is not a burden. But she would see his relation as though it were a relation to the general physical laws, especially that law regarding the degradation of energy. And if she is writing philosophy here, not religious meditation, then this seems badly confused.

The phrase 'necessity of time' is confusing anyway, like saying that I yield to what I cannot alter. I cannot make tomorrow come before tomorrow. As though the 'cannot' were physical and allowed me to add "no matter how I try" (which means nothing).

Weil says (p. 8)[12] that nineteenth-century science "invented a new idea by translating so as to apply to energy that necessity which, together with work, weighs most heavily upon human life," which "is a necessity connected with time itself and consists in the fact that time has a direction." But this is doubly confusing.

We are confused if we think of the law of entropy as expressing the direction of time, and *thus* as expressing some form of necessity. The necessity it has as a law in physics can be seen in the role it plays in physics and in its application there. This has nothing to do with the necessity of "what's done cannot be undone," or in the notion of "perishability." Of course the development of thermodynamics made a great difference to physics. It also led to the growth of statistical mechanics, and we might say this changed the notion of physical necessity, but this is not what Simone Weil refers to.

She is speaking of how a man bears the passage of time, of reveries and evasions, the ways in which we deceive ourselves by reference to the past; or by the difference which "the future" will make, or again, of the importance of "having a past" or "having roots," and so forth.

"We are constantly aging" would suggest: we are growing more decrepit all the while, less capable of work. Or rather, that is what the analogy between the expressions 'the passage of time' and 'the degradation of energy' would suggest. Yet Simone Weil wants the statement "we are always growing older" to hold for young infants as well. And they are not losing vitality by growing older. All that we can say is that with the passage of time they have lived longer.

The illusion that the law of entropy (the degradation of energy) makes plain to us *what* the direction of time is. But even if it tells you "in what direction all things are moving" (if this means anything), this is not the direction in which *time* is moving.

It is only by conflating "time" and entropy that it could seem plausible to make entropy a general feature of all existence. And in other connections Simone Weil sees that we cannot talk this way: in what she says about the idea of a "closed system" in experimental physics, for instance. We may call such a closed system "timeless." But then the second law of thermodynamics is timeless. And it does not explain how that which weighs most heavily on human life is connected with time.

Weil tried, especially in her *Notebooks*, to bring some analogy of this law into an account of moral development and decline, and into her account of decisions and motives. She speaks of "énergie mentale," distinguishing higher and lower forms of psychic energy, or "degradation" or "requalification" of energy when it passes from higher motives to lower, or from lower to higher, the transfer of energy from one level to the other, and so on. Here 'degradation' and 'requalification' are expressions of *value*, as they are not in physics. She is using an analogy: using a *phraseology* taken from thermodynamics, as she is when she speaks of the "mechanism" of the soul, or the mechanism of motives. But the analogy only goes part way, and she does not discuss its limits. Sometimes she seems to be using something like the language of physics when she speaks of the ways in which good and evil "operate" in the soul, the way in which the soul reacts to them, and so on. Think of how suffering and affliction come together in affliction, for instance. But apart from the words, there is nothing here at all analogous to anything in physics. And there is nothing like physical *investigation*—measurement, especially.

To ask about the relation of human beings to the world, or *a* human being in the world in which he is, is to ask something about the value of the world, or the value of the sort of reality that is presented by the scientific account. The relation of this to value. She thought that Greek science had tried to take account of this, to show something about the value of the world, giving an account which showed the beauty (or order) of the world.

If we speak of a man's relation to *necessity*, this can be given only to a very minor extent by Bacon's maxim. This leaves out of account the ways in which human beings are crushed by the forces they understand. Although this point should have been obvious in the conception of the indifference of physical laws to good or evil.

This meant, I suppose, that the relation of a man to the world could not become clear except through the love of God, except in so far as he appreciated the beauty of the world. What then is the relation between what becomes clear through the love of God and what becomes clear through science?

On the other hand, if we said simply that the love of God makes clear the relation of a man to the world, this would be either unintelligible or else obviously false. It raises the question of the relation between what is clear through the love of God and what is clear through the development of science.

To have a love of God, and to have an understanding of one's relation to the world are one and the same thing. (Instead of "relation to the world" we could have said "relation to reality" I suppose.) So one may have an understanding of one's relation to the world without an understanding of science. As most of the great religious teachers and mystics showed.

And there are other ways of representing one's relation to the world, other ways of giving a picture of, or *une image* of, one's relation to the world. Such as those in the Upanishads, perhaps. (This is different from the 1934 view.)

At the same time, Simone Weil occasionally speaks as though the religious believer who does have a true understanding of his relation to the world were like the blind man on the road to Larissa (although somehow this ought not to be right, on her view).

She thinks that science does provide or make possible what she calls *une image du monde*. This is connected with the idea of generality in science, and with the general conception (or conceptions) involved in any form of scientific inquiry, such as the conceptions of *work* and of *energy* in classical mechanics. But she also refers to ways in which a segment of a formal series may present us with an image of the series continuing indefinitely, in this way giving an image, if not of the world, then of something comparable.

But the conception of "an image of the world" remains sketchy in her presentation, and I find it troublesome. (Without it, apparently, one could have no conception of an "order of the world.") It is important when she compares the image of the world provided by science with an image of the world put forward in Buddhist poems, perhaps.

I imagine that one reason why Simone Weil started to write that essay on *La Science et Nous* was just that her whole conception of the relation between thought and reality had changed, or was changing.

Her earlier view, in which the grasp, or 'constatation', of reality came primarily through producing transformations, either experimentally in a laboratory or in practical affairs—in other words, it came by acting upon things and obstacles—for this view, classical science or mechanics would have given a much more adequate account of what the understanding or interpretation of reality could be.

It was as she came to emphasize the importance of love of something, as a precondition of the apprehension of reality, that the idea of a love of the world acquired for her not only an ethical significance (as her earlier adoption of the Stoic *amor fati* had had) but a significance for the theory of knowledge, and hence the idea of the pursuit of science as an attempt to find, recognize, the order of the world. And this (for some reason that is not quite clear) would mean for her the beauty of the world. To understand this I suppose one needs not only a notion of 'equilibrium', but also a notion of 'hiérarchie': the introduction of conceptions of value.

At any rate, she does not seem to remark any special beauty in the "order" portrayed by classical mechanics.

In the *Leçons de Philosophie*, she does not, if I remember, speak about the order of the world at all. It may be she would have thought this was a conception beyond anything we can talk about.

As regards *necessity*: in her later view it is not merely that necessity operates without regard to our needs. The world dominated by the laws of classical mechanics would be one which took no notice of us. But rather that necessity operates without regard to good or evil; in other words, the account of it is given much more in terms of value.

It is in this negative way that she thinks it was described by Plato.

We might say that a different conception of science (as the Greek conception of science was different from the classical one) would naturally have, or include, a different conception of necessity. At the same time, the emphasis on the apprehension of necessity as a way of realizing the difference between reality and fantasy, does remain in her earlier and her later views.

Anne Reynaud's quotation, on page 256: "Le monde est un texte à plusieurs significations, et l'on passe d'une signification à une autre par un travail." (The world is a text with several meanings, and one moves from one meaning to another by work.) Here the importance of *lectures*, which seems to come in to the increasing emphasis upon judgements of value in une connaissance du monde.

There is also the suggestion of *primäre Zeichen* (primary signs) in that passage: Zeichen which would be the same for any language, or for any *travail* or for any *lecture*.

In 1934 her point had been: we can grasp the necessity only of what we can *construct*. On the other hand, reality is what *interferes* with our constructions, appears as something not given in the problem as posed; or at any rate, this is what 'reality' is. But this remains for us an "accident," I suppose—something which we do not understand—until we are able to create a model for it, so to speak. (For Plato's 'necessity' I do not think it would have been possible to create a model.) At any rate the position was that of understanding necessity through the construction of dynamic models. (For Plato, necessity could not be understood in this way.)

Weil wants to clarify or to understand the relation of thought and reality.

She wants to show or to understand how it is that we distinguish between reality and illusion or between reality and dreaming.

She would say, probably, that thinking is an activity in the mind. But it is distinguished from dreaming or imagining by a certain form, which she calls method. This is clearest in solving mathematical problems, but it is seen clearly also in the development of hypotheses and experiments in physics. There are different forms of reasoning, and there are different methods, some appropriate to one sort of problem and not to others. But in all reasoning and all method there is a recognition of *order*.

Order depends on our having language, if only because language makes it possible for us to recognize temporal sequence.

"Order is something which unfolds in time, and depends on a relationship between successive operations. Without language there is no recollection: so, an operation which has taken place would no longer exist" (*Lectures*, p. 69).[13]

In her earlier view, up to 1934 or 1935, anyway, Weil emphasized the relation and the contrast between what we have through *language* and what we have through *action* (bodily movement), especially in regard to our relations to things. In our actions, the relations which we have to things are determined by our needs. And we do not ourselves decide or determine what our needs shall be. This may be decided, for example, by the circumstances and the obstacles which I happen to meet. If I act from a need for food, I may find myself in danger, and driven by a need of another sort. My needs may determine what I experience in things, or what I find out about them. But there is no "objective" order in what I have in this way. "Les besoins se succèdent au hasard." (The sequence of our needs is haphazard.)

Relations established by thought and language—relations of *order* or of necessary sequences of operations—are independent of time. Even if the sequence be a temporal sequence, we are not describing actual happenings, but the *formal* dependence of operations. If we follow (apply) such an order, we are not following (applying) an hypothesis.

Action may be methodical; it may be initiated and guided by calculation and attention to order. But when the steps in my performance (action) succeed one another, this is not independent of circumstances, and it may always be interrupted by circumstances I had not foreseen.

I am acting when I perform an experiment, or when I carry out any project.

Relations of thought and reality are shown especially in the relations between thought (method) and action. What does not come from pure thought, what appears as an *obstacle*, is reality.

The relation of the world to God conceived on Kantian lines: the compatibility between the world of ends and *this* world (which is a world of means) (p. 193).

"La croyance en l'existence de Dieu, cela signifie pour Kant qu'il n'y a pas incompatibilité entre le monde des moyens et celui des fins" (p. 194). (For Kant, belief in God's existence means that there is no incompatibility between the world of means and that of ends.)

Would this be comparable with what she says in *Intuitions Pré-Chrétiennes*, p. 152, of "La nécessité étant médiatrice entre la matière et Dieu" (necessity's being the mediator between matter and God)?

This "compatibility" is not something shown by mechanics. There is nothing in the mechanical picture of the world to suggest it. *Nota bene*: in neither of these conceptions is there any sense of God as *Amour*.

The Greeks.

The "theological" character of mathematical necessity.

This is something which she had not had in her earlier view, where the suggestion was rather that necessity and order is something that comes *from us*.

The importance also of *contradiction*—the sense of contradiction both as a "mark of reality" and also as the occasion or place for contemplation. Here there is no sense of transforming constraint into an obstacle and discovering ways of dealing with it.

The notion of unconditional necessity (impossibility, *n'importe quoi*) and the paradigm of this in morality.

The difference (apparently) between 'unconditional' and 'unlimited': "necessity" as a "limit."

This is still very different from the "necessity" or "gravity" to which we are subject in time and circumstance. (This use of the term 'gravity' for the *general* character of natural happening, suggests Newtonian mechanics. Yet 'necessity' does not mean just what it does there.)

The fact that material masses can be beautiful, or that a human being (a human body) can live and move in ways that are saintly— this is not something that classical mechanics can explain or make intelligible. No more than it can explain or help us to understand the degradation or near destruction of the soul in affliction. (The question "why?")

But to say that classical mechanics "cannot explain these" does not mean that the *theories* of classical mechanics are shown to be defective here, or perhaps, that this is a problem demanding other techniques. For the trouble is in the sense of 'account for'. And it would be a mistake to call this ("Why do such things happen?") a *problem* in the sense in which we do speak of problems in mechanics.

Notes

A compilation of remarks taken from a letter to Peter Winch dated 1 November 1968; two letters to M. O'C. Drury dated 6 March and 18 March 1969; and Notes dated 12.4.64, 10.12.68 and 10.2.69. This material repeats some of the points made in the previous essays on science. Rhees kept coming back to these issues because of their complexity, and we have assumed that the reader will benefit from doing so too. (Ed)

1. Published as *Lectures on Philosophy*, trans. Hugh Price, Cambridge: Cambridge University Press, 1978. *Leçons de Philosophie*, Paris: Librairie Plon, 1959.

2. *The Need for Roots*, trans. A. F. Wills, London: Routledge and Kegan, Paul, 1952.

3. In *Sur la Science*, Paris: Gallimard, 1966, pp. 121–76, translated as "Classical Science and After" in Simone Weil, *On Science, Necessity, and the Love of God*, ed. and trans. Richard Rees, Oxford University Press, 1968, pp. 3–43.

4. *Lectures on Philosophy*, op. cit.

5. "But when one has understood that the lines drawn by the geometer and the objects of the physicist's observation or experiment are limitations of mathematical ideas, one has still learned very little. One still does not know what that relation is which for want of a better term is described as imitation." Simone Weil, "Classical Science and After," in *On Science, Necessity, and the Love of God*, trans. and ed. by Richard Rees, Oxford University Press, 1968, p. 34).

"Mais quand on a compris que les lignes tracées par le géomètre, que les choses objets de l'observation ou de l'expérimentation du physicien, sont des imitations des notions mathématiques, on a compris bien peu de chose encore. Car on ignore en quoi consiste ce rapport que l'on peut nommer, faute de mieux, imitation," "La Science et Nous" in *Sur la Science*, Paris: Gallimard, 1966, p. 164.

6. You would not be looking for me if you had not already found me; do not worry.

7. Love is not consolation; it is light.

8. The void.

From Notes dated 10.2.69

9. Compare *On Science, Necessity and the Love of God*, p. 178, with the above translation by Rhees. The original reads: "Le mécanisme de la nécessité se transpose à tous les niveaux en restant semblable à lui-même dans la matière brute, dans les plantes, dans les animaux, dans les peuples, dans les âmes. Regardé du point où nous sommes, selon notre perspective, il est tout à fait aveugle. Mais si nous transportons notre coeur hors de nous-mêmes, hors de l'univers, hors de l'espace et du temps, là où est notre Père, et si de là nous regardons ce mécanisme, il apparaît tout autre. Ce qui semblait nécessité devient obéissance. La matière est entière passivité, et par suite entière obéissance à la volonté de Dieu. Elle est pour nous un parfait modèle. Par sa parfaite obéissance la matière mérite d'être aimée par ceux qui aiment son Maître" (*Pensées*, p. 97).

10. "L'homme ne peut jamais sortir de l'obéissance à Dieu. Une créature ne peut pas ne pas obéir. Le seul choix offert à l'homme comme créature intelligente et libre, c'est de désirer l'obéissance ou de ne pas la désirer. (. . .) S'il la désire, il reste soumis à la nécessité mécanique, mais une nécessité nouvelle s'y surajoute, une nécessité constituée par les lois propres . . . à travers lui parfois presque malgré lui" (*Pensées*, p. 98).

11. "Le consentement est une folie, la folie propre à l'homme. (. . .) L'amour que Saint Jean portart à celui qui était son ami et son seigneur, quand il était incliné sur la pointrine pendant la Cène, c'est cet amour même que nous devons porter à l'enchaînement mathématique de causes et d'effets qui, de temps à autre, fait de nous une espèce de bouillie informe. Manifestement cela est fou." "Descente," pp. 148–50.

12. ". . . elle inventa une notion nouvelle en traduisant, pour l'appliquer à l'énergie, la nécessité qui, avec celle de travailler, pèse le plus lourdement sur la vie humaine. Cette nécessité tient au temps lui-même et consiste en ce qu'il est dirigé. . . ." *La Science et Nous*, p. 128.

13. "L'ordre est quelque chose qui se déroule dans le temps, qui repose sur un rapport entre les opérations successives. Sans langage, pas de souvenir: donc, une operation passée n'existerait plus" (*Leçons de Philosophie*, p. 52).

PART THREE

REFLECTIONS ON ETHICS AND RELIGION

CHAPTER NINE

LOVE

———————

PURITY

The more I read Simone Weil, the more I admire her. The *Notebooks* contain conflicting views sometimes, as you would expect. I do not know that all the remarks are equally good. Often I see better the sense of a remark when I have come back to it a number of times, so I should not want to say definitely that they are uneven. But it would be surprising if they were all equally good, and I hardly think she would have said they were. Some of them I think wonderful; most of her remarks about beauty and about contemplation, for instance.

"Beauty: a fruit which we look at without trying to seize it. The same with an affliction which we contemplate without drawing back."[1]

She says that to nourish those that are hungry is a form of contemplation.

At the same time, there are certain of her ideas which come back again and again, and which one must call central in what she writes, which do seem to raise difficulties. Perhaps most of them are connected with what she says about "le vide," but I am not sure.

She often says things like, "If you love anyone, then always think of him as though he were dead." (For example, *Notebooks* I, p. 218: "To love whilst remaining detached. To endure the thought that those we love, on whom we think lovingly, are mortal, are perhaps dead at the very moment we are thinking of them—this is an anguish. . . . We should never think of a human being, unless he is by our side, without thinking that he is perhaps dead."[2] I think there are other passages more exactly as I first put it.) In this way you make sure that the love be *pure*, and you are sure of detachment. If in your love for someone you are possessed by the thought of seeing him again—by thoughts of what the future may bring, and of the joy of his company—then the love is not pure. It is not purely a love of *him*: it is contaminated by imagination. Perhaps she would say that your love is then not concentrated on him; you have not disregarded yourself. Or she might say: Your love is not a love of him; it is a love of life.

In much of this I can see what she means. And I think she is making a point which is important. But there are consequences which make me think she is mistaken or confused in some way.

It would seem to follow from what she says that if you love someone, you ought not to be concerned about what may happen to him while he is alive. You ought not even to care whether in his life he is going to come nearer to God or to be degraded.

She may well say that you ought not to be concerned about his worldly achievements. It will not matter whether these are frustrated by death or not. But they are not the whole story. And there are other considerations to make one say it *does* matter whether he dies now or later. Suppose Simone Weil had died before she had the revelation that she did?

"What would the miser lose if his treasure were stolen from him?" "What would you lose if the person you love were taken from you by death?" You would love him none the less, and your sense of his reality would be just as great.

She makes what I think a wonderful remark about Christ and the relatives of the dead Lazarus. Christ was not disturbed when he saw the sickness of Lazarus, nor when he saw his death. Only when he saw Mary and those with her were in tears. It was then that he groaned deeply within himself. (Because of their shallowness and their want of understanding.)

"This sickness is not unto death." I think I know something of what he meant. But I do not think one can argue as Simone Weil does.

Let me ask you again: suppose she herself had died before she came to know Christ or had seen Christ. She cannot argue that she would have had this knowledge in eternity anyway; for on her view there will be no 'she' (Simone Weil) in eternity. This is one reason why she wants to eliminate the 'I' as much as possible here and now. This is one of the points on which I suspect there is some confusion, and I suspect that Kierkegaard's view had more reality.

She cannot really argue that life, the *temporal* life of Simone Weil, does not matter. I think this would be blasphemous even on her view. And if it implies—and does it not?—that what happens in her life does not matter, then it would contradict all she says about the difference between spirituality (purity) and degradation.

So I think that if I love someone, I ought to hope that things will go one way for him, and not another way. And often this may mean that I ought to hope that he has not died and that he will not die. (After the death of Lazarus, the case is different. It is the question whether one should mourn him. And however this be answered, it is different from the question whether one should be rid of all hopes and fears for him while he is living.)

Sometimes Simone Weil speaks as though *all* attachment were something like the attachment of a miser for his treasure. But of course she cannot hold to this line, since it makes nonsense of charity, of compassion, and so on.

She would say, I suppose, that I ought not to let my love of any creature come between me and my love of God. She can make this consistent with the teaching of St. John, by holding that to love my neighbour or to love my brother, I should love as God does, and this means to love all creatures equally. (I believe that St. John of the Cross says somewhere that you can never be sure that God does not hate you. And Simone Weil also says in some places that she cannot believe that God loves her personally, although he may love her as a creature. I suppose St. John of the Cross meant: you can never be sure that you are not damned.) She seems to suggest that if I loved all creatures equally, or that if I loved the world as a whole, this would not be attachment to the world; perhaps because it would not be the operation of "gravity" or of "necessity," which impels me to love one person or one place more than another.

Once again it seems to me that she is mistaken. And yet I think she is emphasizing something which is true. It is true, I think, that my love is pure in the measure in which it does not consider the effects; does not consider what it will bring, what fruits it may bear, and so on. And I can see the sense in arguing that if my love is pure, that I should be able to bear to be separated from the person I love.

Love is made pure by the contemplation of beauty. And the contemplation of beauty frees me from any wish to possess. If my love were predominantly a desire to possess, then it would be like the miser's love for his gold.

But really it is not as simple as that. If I do not want to be separated from the person I love, this need not mean that I want to possess him (or her). Although it *may* be that. (We do not need to consider the special sense of 'possessing a woman' here.) It may be that the thought of having her for my own, having her at my side, and so on, is more important than anything else, that is, more important than the spiritual intercourse which is love or friendship. If that were so, then I agree that the lover would not be much different from the miser. But what makes the miser so strange is that there is no such spiritual intercourse with his money. He cannot learn from it as one learns in love and friendship. And although he may make sacrifices to keep it, he does not make sacrifices for *it*; he does not have a love for *it* in the way in which you love the woman who is yours, and for whom you make every sacrifice. What the miser loves is his *possession* of the money (but this is still badly expressed).

There are passages in which Simone Weil recognizes the difference between a miser's love and the love of man and wife, clearly enough. As of course she would. In "La Connaissance Surnaturelle" there is a wonderful prayer; so far as I know it is the only fairly long prayer she wrote. It is a prayer which is very revealing, since it asks—with the terrible sincerity which much of her writing has—"that I may be insensible to every sort of grief and of joy, and incapable of love for anyone, for any thing, not even for myself, like old people who are completely paralysed and insane." She goes on at some length, and she makes the whole thing deeply beautiful.

> Example of prayer.
> Saying to God:
> Father, in the name of Christ, grant me this:
> That, just as with someone who is completely paralysed, my will may find no expression in bodily movement, however rudimentary. That, like someone who is totally blind, deaf, and deprived of the three other senses, I may be incapable of having any sensations whatever. That, like a village idiot who does not know how to count or read, and has never even learnt to speak, I may be unable to string together even the simplest thoughts.
> That I may be insensible to every sort of grief and of joy, and incapable of any love for anyone, for any thing, not even for myself, like a silly old fool.
> Father, in the name of Christ, do grant me this. That my body may move with perfect suppleness, or stand still with perfect rigidity,

and in unswerving conformity to your will. That my hearing, sight, taste, smell, touch, may receive the perfectly faithful stamp of your creation. That my mind may, in the fullness of lucidity, combine all its ideas in perfect conformity with your truth. That I may experience, as intensely and purely as possible, the whole spectrum of sorrow and of joy. That my love for God may be a flame, completely consumed by God's love. That all this may be forced from me, consumed by God, transformed in the body of Christ, and fed to the unfortunate whose bodies and souls lack any kind of nourishment. And that I may be a paralysed, blind, deaf, and senile old fool.

Father, bring about this transformation now, in the name of Christ; and even though I am asking this with imperfect faith, hear this request as if it had been made in perfect faith.

Father, since you are the Good and I am the inadequate, take this body and soul from me and make them your own, and for all eternity let not remain anything of me but this appropriation—or rather: nothingness—itself.

Such words can have any real virtue only if they are dictated by the Holy Spirit. One may not ask for such things by one's own will. It is a point one reaches in spite of oneself. In spite of oneself, one consents to it. One does not consent voluntarily. One consents with a violence exercised by one's entire soul. But the consent is entire and without reserve, given by a single movement of one's whole being.

Is it from this that the metaphor of marriage comes? The relation between God and the soul is like that of a husband with a wife who is still a virgin, on their wedding night. Marriage is a violation by consent. And similarly the union of the soul with God. The soul feels cold, and does not feel that it loves God. It does not itself know whether if it did not love it would not consent. The conjugal union turns the human personality into a simple intermediary between its flesh and God. Other souls love God as a woman loves her lover. But the loves of lovers are not everlasting. Only man and wife are one single flesh for ever.

(But all these spiritual phenomena are completely beyond my grasp. I know nothing about them. They are reserved for those beings who, to begin with, possess the elementary moral virtues. I am speaking off the top of my hat here. In spite of this, I am not even capable of sincerely telling myself that I am doing so.)[3]

I want to emphasise her insistence:

"Such words can have any real virtue only if they are dictated by the Holy Spirit. One may not ask for such things by one's own will. It is a point one reaches in spite of oneself. In spite of oneself, one consents. Not that one consents by giving up the struggle. One consents with a violence exercised by one's entire soul upon one's entire soul. But the consent is entire and without reserve, given by a single movement of the whole being."

I also want to emphasise the wonderful parenthesis:

"But all these spiritual phenomena are completely beyond my grasp. I know nothing about them. They are reserved for those beings who, to begin with, possess the elementary moral virtues. I am speaking off the top of my hat here. In spite of this, I am not even capable of sincerely telling myself that I am doing so."

You would know that she could see that. And yet her doctrine of detachment and of obliteration of the self distorted other things she said, as it led finally to her own death.

"Cut all attachment to this world." I think this is evil. (I say this although I admire her and her life as I have hardly admired anyone.) I think it is a flight from responsibility. And it disregards the dependence of other people on you.

Something the same can be said of much that she says of uprooting oneself from one's culture and one's heritage, because these are a hindrance to "nudity" and purity. Once again I think she is saying something which is deeply important. It has to do, of course, with the refusal to "be someone," and so it is connected with the idea of intellectual probity. But in her hands it also goes to ways which are, I believe, in a deep sense evil.

DETACHMENT

I do not find it hard to see what she means by "Always think of one you love as though he were dead." The remark is important because it is closely connected with her ideas of 'the void' and of 'the "I"'. A large part of the remarks included in *Gravity and Grace* is concerned with these. And it is in this matter of the void and of the "I" that she is most obviously in a different position from Kierkegaard. She differs from him in the way she writes, too. And it is the way she writes—the person she is—that speaks in what she says.

Her understanding of suffering, and of the difference between suffering and 'affliction' (malheur), goes deeper than anything I know.

Some of what she says about it seems to come from a very deep conviction, which she held in her early days, before she tried to write of religion, when she was a declared atheist. For example, in some of her early political writings she speaks strongly against the idea of removing or alleviating suffering. I think she would have said at that time, too, that what matters is not whether a man suffers but *how* he suffers. Just as in her later writings she used to say that the distinction between suffering and joy was not the important one, since there are forms of each—forms of suffering and forms of joy—which are ennobling and forms which are degrading, and it is here in the difference between what ennobles and what degrades that we have the only important difference. Joy can be degrading as easily as suffering (the miser's joy in his money), or perhaps more easily.

She was bitter about the conditions in which workers in mass-production factories have to work. They become exhausted and stupefied by their work, which can mean nothing to them, and they are subjected to constant humiliation by those in charge. But these are not the chief evils in themselves. They are evil because, in these conditions and in this state of exhaustion, one is driven to suppress all interests in the work and all decent motives. One has to change one's rate or way of working or type of work at once, at the command of the foreman, under conditions of fatigue when an order like that may seem almost unbearable.

> In these circumstances one depends so much on the foremen that one cannot help being afraid of them, and—once more I confess it unwillingly—one needs a constant effort to keep from falling into servility. In the third place, this discipline (of the factory) appeals to no motives except the most sordid interests—the scale of cash paid—and fear. If you let such motives take an important place, you defile yourself. If you suppress them, if you become indifferent to cash and to threats, then you make yourself incapable of the completely passive obedience which is required, and incapable of repeating the movements of the job in the cadence which is imposed; an incapacity that is promptly punished by hunger.

And she has much more on these lines.

But even in her early attention to Marx, she never could tolerate the Marxist idea of 'progress'; or rather, the idea of progress which had been given special vitality by the French Revolution. She thought that idea was nonsense.

It is something the same when she writes at a later stage that "the amount of suffering in the world is constant," and will not be changed by the love of God or the growth of religion. It is in no sense a consequence of sin, as we see in the fact that Christ was no more free from suffering than the most afflicted sinner.

The depth with which she writes of this, and the freedom from every shade of self-assertion or consideration of effect—what she herself calls the "nakedness" of the style she strove for—brings her into everything she says. And more than half of what one learns, one learns from her: what she says is illuminating because she is saying it.

With this there are also certain limits—questions she disregarded because they did not belong to her. The suffering of which she speaks most often, the suffering from which one can learn, the suffering which may open one to the grace of God, is the suffering which belongs to one as a creature. She speaks of the portrayal of such suffering in the Book of Job and in the Greek tragedies and in *King Lear*. On the other hand, she gives little attention to the suffering which is often the relation of people to one another—especially of those who love one another, which is the stuff of tragedy. Is this because she imagined that all such difficulties could be solved by "detachment"? At any rate, I hardly think they interested her. She speaks often of *physical* suffering, and also the suffering which comes from the exercise of brutality, and from the exercise of "force" as in war. I suppose this was part of the subjection of human beings to "gravity." And in one sense it is impersonal: what I suffer belongs to my condition as a creature, and it is something to which any other might be subject. She also speaks of the way in which, at the moment I know my sin for what it is, the sin is suffering (and then, like all suffering, it is a way to the knowledge of God). And similarly with bereavement, which may also lead to knowledge of God, and on this account it may be an occasion for gratitude to God. ("The love of God is pure when joy and grief inspire gratitude *in equal measure*.") But the situation of a man and woman whose marriage is breaking up, she *never* considers, as far as I know. I am thinking especially of the case where it is breaking although they love one another (it would not be so terrible otherwise), and although the break is not the result of any clear wrong done by either partner. Eugene O'Neill wrote about situations near to this in some of his plays. "If only they had loved one another enough. . . ." Good Christ, if only they *hadn't* loved one another. She always fought shy of intimate friendship herself. And she thought of love as a distraction and an interference (as in all conscience it is). But this went with a more general tendency: the tendency to ignore the relations between two persons or two individuals which are the relations of just *these* individuals.

She admired *Antigone*, and I can see why. For one thing, it is the devotion of a woman to someone who is dead, and the view of this is also a longing for the other world. On occasions she speaks of Electra's recognition of her brother. But the relation between Electra and her mother, which I think Giraudoux[4] has portrayed wonderfully, she does not consider; and I can imagine her shrugging her shoulders and showing no interest.

The relation of man and woman. The relation of parent and child. Relations without which there would be no life. Relations in which love goes deep and breaks people. I do not think these are ever considered in religion. Christ never considers them. The love of one's neighbour, of which he speaks, is the love of a stranger in distress, who will never be seen again.

Strange, in one way. Because the tragedy which comes from the love of parents and children is so often a theme of Jewish stories.

The *bereavement* of the beloved, and the bereavement of children—yes, they consider this. And this does perhaps make one aware, sometimes, of one's relation to God. In the hopelessness of the other situations, it is not so clear.

SUFFERING

Simone Weil had a tendency to a kind of pantheism. She was strongly interested in Spinoza when she was a student. And I imagine there are traces of his influence. Her view of individuals may come partly from him.

She always speaks of the need to think of her own suffering in a *general* way: as a revelation of the misery of the human state. And her clarity towards the suffering of others seems to have been towards them as 'others' more often than as this person or that. In her political writings she came more and more to insist on the importance of individuals, in opposition to the doctrines of the Marxists. This is one thing which I like especially. But she is thinking here of individuals in general—*any* individual. Like the Christian neighbour.

In the *Notebooks* she says, for instance, "Whatever may happen to me, how could I ever think my affliction too great—since the teeth of the affliction and the abasement to which it condemns me makes possible my knowledge of human misery: knowledge which is the gateway, the passage for all true wisdom?"[5] And then on the next page: "Be nothing, so that you may be in your true place in the whole."[6] And a little lower down on the same page she speaks of the need to know "that human misery is a constant and irreducible quantity, and is as great in each man as it can be; and that the magnitude (of the suffering) comes from a single God, *in such a way as there is an identity between one man and another.*"[7] The underscoring is mine, not hers. I wonder if you see the resemblance to Spinoza.

Am I wrong to emphasize this? I think I am. For: (1) She differs from Spinoza on more points than she has in common with him. Her idea of Creation as a renunciation of the world by God, for instance. So that the only way a creature can come to God is by following him, that is, through renouncing the world. (2) Even where she seems to speak with the voice of Spinoza, she has important reasons for what she says—reasons which have no connexion with anything Spinoza said.

A religious person must ignore much in human affairs, must ignore many human difficulties. A religious person who writes about evil and suffering must ignore many forms of evil and of suffering. So must anyone else, of course, depending on the angle from which he speaks.

Simone Weil is speaking of that love of other creatures which is the same as the love of God. It is this which required humility (and she has much to say on this). And it is a love of them simply *as* God's creatures. This means: as illustrations of human misery. There is something religious about the love which does not belong to any other. The sense of what it is to be a creature of God. The love that goes with the recognition that this is God's creation. The love that is compassion.

Strange, to think of the love of God as compassion. But this is a sense—however hidden and obstructed—a sense of God's love: his love of those for whom I feel compassion. It is only in this way that I become aware of his love: only through the compassion which *is* the knowledge that these are God's creatures. To be aware of God and to be aware of his love are one and the same.

God's love for his creatures will not put an end to their suffering. God's love for his Son.

She distinguished the person from the "impersonal" in any human being. And she speaks of the impersonal as "the sacred." It is impersonal in the sense in which there is something impersonal or anonymous about any great work of art. To know what is truly great in *King Lear* or in the Book of Job is to know what is not "the expression of an author."

The beauty of the world is the revelation of God. But not as it might show its authorship.

And she would think of God as neither person nor impersonal. (This is important.) To love God, I must get rid of what is personal in me. Just as I must if I am to show compassion. Otherwise the "compassion" is vanity and evil. (It is what she calls the "false divinity" which men have assumed since Adam. The false divinity which comes between them and God.)

This is one reason why she insists on detachment as she does. I must not seek to make anything mine. Not even the exercise of compassion should be mine. Submission; obedience; passivity. The compassion which I cannot help. Compassion which is also suffering. Suffering as obedience to the will of God. An obedience which I can show only by ceasing to be 'I'. Only through the love of God.

Compassion which is also suffering. Simone Weil thought she ought literally to suffer in the way those suffered for whom she felt compassion; otherwise the compassion would not be pure.

Her insight into evil is as remarkable as her perception in other matters. But I do not see (yet) that she has made plain the relation of evil and God.

She says more than once that there is no such thing as egoism. I think there is something important in this, and I am inclined to agree with her. What is called egoism is often the attachment to one's own comforts, or the desire for recognition, and so on. But she places great importance in the distinction between what is elevated and what is base. And again I welcome this way of putting it (even if the special allusions of 'high' and 'low' in connexion with 'gravity' are less appealing to me).

Granting that the door to all wisdom lies in the knowledge of suffering, she says that there are sufferings in which suffering is degrading and shuts one off from knowledge of God. I am sure this is right. But . . . does it fit with the rest of her view? Why should this degradation not also furnish a knowledge of God? And if it did, should it not bring us nearer to God, so that we should welcome it?

Weil does say that if it were not for evil, we could never be persuaded to renounce the world. She also has the characteristic remark (in the *Notebooks*), "To have much sin is an advantage, in so far as it keeps one from looking on natural virtue as a form of misery equivalent to sin." Here "natural virtue" is the exhausting labour to which everyone is, or should be, compelled. 'Should be'—that is, none will be perfect unless he is. This again is very important, in view of the attitude to labour and the exhaustion which it brings which some writers have suggested.

But this by itself would not make sin into good fortune. Still less would sin bring one nearer to God. She speaks of it rather as "solitude of man. Distance from God." (But then in the same passage, she goes on to speak of it as "a condition of decreation," which is the same point, that without evil there would be no renunciation of the world.) Is it stupid to ask, "Well, without evil why *should* there be? And if there were no need to renounce the world, how is there need for evil to make us renounce it?"

She speaks of the will to power as evil, for instance. And also of the evil of imagination which seeks to find consolation for suffering. But these evils . . . how do they stand in the knowledge of God?

She also has very interesting remarks on the difference between suffering with understanding and suffering without understanding, with the suggestion that it is the want of understanding that may make suffering degrading.

TEMPORALITY

"Think of the beloved as though he (she) were dead." This is meant to be detachment. But is it? Would not one's thoughts be more than ever for an opportunity to see and speak to the loved one? "If she could only return for fifteen minutes, I'd sell my soul to have it."

And with this goes the wish to die oneself. This may have some idea of joining the loved one, but it need not: it may be simply the wish to be as she is, to die. Perhaps Simone Weil would approve of this. But I cannot see that it is detachment.

She thinks of 'I' as temporal: as what one is in the world, connected with hopes and fears for what may come. She herself thinks of hope in a different sense.

Kierkegaard's notion of *freedom*. Connexion of this with her notion of detachment. The loss of freedom through the dread of evil, or the dread of good (dread of freedom). Compare what Kierkegaard says of prayer and 'possibility' in *Purity of Heart*.

'Detachment' and the sort of freedom which Spinoza sought. How far was this anything like what Kierkegaard meant? Hardly much, I should imagine.

Kierkegaard and purity of heart. How far is the purity of which Simone Weil writes—pure love, for instance—similar to this? The devotion which is a wish for death (the wish of the abandoned lover is only superficially like this).

L'acceptation de la mort. Certainly the fear of death is evil. But is not the fear of life also evil? Why does she not speak of l'acception de la vie? (The voluptuary does not accept life.) It is almost as though she thought this *must* mean devotion to the world, or becoming a voluptuary. Which for Kierkegaard would be despair (*Either/Or*).

"Know that they are mortal." The beauty of the cherry blossoms lies partly in their fragility. Yes, but not *only* in that; it lies in their *blossoming*, in what they are.

"I think I must love wrongly; otherwise things would not happen in this way to me" (*Notebooks*, Vol. I, p. 206).[8] Does this not mean that *all* love is evil? Compare in this connexion: "When a thing is perfectly beautiful, as soon as we fix our attention upon it, it represents unique and single beauty" (*Notebooks*, Vol. I, pp. 244–45).[9]

(How does her position stand in relation to Robert Frost's "I take my incompleteness with the rest . . ."? Which means, I suppose, inter alia: "I know I am not God.")

"Striving to be God-like. To love as God loves, for instance." Does this mean kicking against one's existence as a creature?

Simone Weil distinguishes between suffering—human misery—and evil. Human misery is just existence as creatures. But she says that without evil one could never renounce the world, which is almost a way of being thankful for evil. And the importance of renouncing the world—that is, creation, suggests that the world *is* evil. One might almost question whether she did believe in the incarnation. Or whether, for her, the incarnation appeared in the crucifixion and nowhere else.

She insists on the beauty of the world. But she sees this as something that awakens the need for detachment, and, for herself, a wish to leave the world (whose beauty she soils). There is something wrong and evil here.

Unwilling to accept herself—surely a false reading of humility.

"Le Christ m'a prise." (Christ has taken possession of me.) None can look on the face of God and live. The vision of the Grail and the wish to die.

LOVE

Simone Weil and the relation between love of God and love of others. She had a terribly vivid sense of the sufferings of others, where this meant (1) physical suffering, (2) suffering injustice—humiliation. She emphasises that Christ was suffering the punishment of a criminal. The sufferings of slaves who were not related as human beings but as "things" (sometimes seeming to suggest that their crucifixion was of a piece with this).

But she has little sense of the suffering of the sinner who is conscious of his sins. Does she anywhere speak of the suffering of Judas? "What is your torment?" (Quel est ton tourment?) [Hell as thinking one is in paradise when one is not.]

Weil does not seem to have known what despair was—to the extent that Kierkegaard did (cf. Lenau). She was keenly aware of her shortcomings. And she knew that these kept her from doing what she might have wanted to do. What she calls her *sins* concerning the political situation before 1939—pacifism especially—were not sins at all: they were errors. She may have wondered how she came to cling to these, and may have found the reason in certain "attachments."

There is something characteristic of her that she should reproach herself for this in the same way as for other of her "sins." Often it was for having failed to utilize the gifts which God had given her: once again, for having failed in an achievement. This is fundamentally different from having failed as a person. And she seems to have had little understanding of this.

I think this went with her barren ideas about friendship. And I do not see how she could have had but a limited understanding of tragedy.

I almost want to say that she did not love human beings at all. This (statement of mine) will not do; when one remembers her reactions to the events in Spain. (Why did it take so long for these reactions to come to the surface or to become dominant?) Her insistence that *individuals* are important, that political parties and "le social" are evil because they destroy what is native to the individual—this lasted on to her very final writings. Even what she says about "detachment" and asceticism she did not want to make universally applicable, because she recognized that human beings are differently constituted, and what might be fatal for one ('il tombe', he is falling—what did she understand by this?) would not be so for another. It is a matter of saving oneself—or of its being made possible to save oneself—from *degradation*. And certainly this conception is prominent through her writings.

And yet, how far did it go beyond this: that human beings are differently constituted? This seems to think of them as having to fulfil the same tasks, each in his way and according to his powers. She is generally thinking of the performance of a particular sort of task and considers the "economy of psychical energy" which different individuals may need for it. "Pursuit of the good is one thing" (Kierkegaard).

There is a way of speaking which suggests this: when we say "He found life too much for him." Compare St. Paul's phrases about having to run a course (in which, apparently, you are competing with others, and "there is only one prize").

The difficulty of talking about morality in general terms. (To analyse is not to force something into a form.) Most artists and writers have rejected this.

Think of someone like Hardy's Jude. Or Tolstoy's Anna Karenina. The mess a man has got himself into. The futility—or misunderstanding—of casuistry, which seems to suggest that he could have found the answer in the book.

It is not only that human beings are differently constituted. They have their own problems. They make their own false steps, but also do things foul or contemptible. There is a special sort of understanding of this, which great writers may show. This is something different from being able to look affliction in the face.

In some ways this is connected with love and friendship. Compare the sins of Brutus and Judas. And I am thinking of *earthly* love here: Antigone may not be the best illustration.

I am trying to find some connexion for this point about Simone Weil. She feared friendship, because she exposed herself to wounding to which she would not otherwise have been liable—which otherwise she would not have had to fear. (The interest in friendship centred in herself?)

Workers in a factory who had to suffer privation and humiliation and frustration: from these she could understand that even a wish or attempt to be kind would meet with bitterness and repulsion. Simone Weil would not herself have suffered any wound that went very deep here. She was not worried about wounded vanity. And her wish to help would have been genuine and free from vanity anyway.

But her love for another person could never go deep enough to forgive the sort of hurt that comes in friendship. (Think of parents and children.) She lacked the understanding, then (I suppose), which would go with this. An understanding of a certain sort of human failing—or of vileness. It may be different to ascribe this sort of evil (which may seem "gratuitous"?) to la pesanteur.

Once again, the attempt to identify the love of men and the love of God. "All you can really (or unconditionally) love in men is their love of God."

Then you hardly love them as men.

"Pursuit of the good is one thing": There is some gross ambiguity in this as it stands. For Simone Weil it was connected with the view that the love of God is the only thing "unconditionally" worthwhile.

If it were said that something—say study or friendship—is not *unconditionally* good, Simone Weil would take this to be a disparagement of it, apparently. With what reason, I cannot see. It seems to be in line with Kant's remarks about "the good will." Does Camus have some criticisms relevant to this?

Affliction and compassion. It was generally the affliction of those in poverty and labourers, especially slaves, the most disenfranchised and unjustly treated *class* of human beings—which she considered.

She does not seem to have found it natural to believe that there could be deep affliction or deep suffering of someone who did not belong to the class of the downtrodden. Compare, "The healthy need no physician."

". . . there is faith in unconditional love. This is 'the love of that which does not exist,' which is not at the mercy of death, and which neither illness can ruin, nor whim prevent us from cherishing. If it does not exist, it is because we find a security in this negation which is lacking from that which exists."[10]

"The vulnerability of precious things is beautiful because it is a hallmark of existence. (. . .) Thus, the soul's vulnerability to coldness, to hunger . . ."[11]

The idea that the realization that human love is exposed to blemishes and to changes, and especially "that it is not stronger than death," that this realization must be shocking or "horrible" to the lover. Presumably because of the thought that love is eternal; his profession of a love that is undying; his conviction that his love is really pure and holy, whatever defilement it may suffer at his hands.

This does prevent a difficulty for any account of love. But she does not try to solve it: to see how the conviction that "love is eternal" does fit together with, say, the jealousy which is often part of love. She does not recognize, or pay attention to, anyway, the problems and difficulties that belong to love. She does not see how a successful passage through these may add to the value of love, especially, that they give it its character as this love. This is what she misses. Just as she misses the distinction between desire and affection. I feel that this is not an accident, but that it is connected with other views of hers.

Compare her admiration for the love of the troubadours as something "*impossible*"—seeing its value and beauty in this.

Phallic rights as an admiration of chastity. (Does chastity mean the denial of love?)

The individual character of the love of Romeo and Juliet, or of Antony and Cleopatra. Growth, or development, being something (besides consumption) in the lives of lovers. Goethe's recognition of this: Faust and Margarete—the fruit or creation which love brings to their lives. (Why the emphasis on *consumption* in Simone Weil?) Love as something that gives, rather than as something that consumes. And this giving cannot be anonymous. It is something which only the beloved *can* give: no other "well disposed" person could do it. She is thinking of *seduction*, apparently, and little else.

Her religious ideal would require that my love of one person should have no character which did not belong also to my love of another. Then of course it *is* anonymous. It is not something which grows and gets its character from the love it *receives* from the other person. In other words, one would not love him as a human being with human failings: and your love would not include acceptance (or forgiveness) of wrong he may have done you.

It is remarkable that she never considers love of parents and children, although she regards love of God as in some sense—or as analogous to—love of a father.

'WRONG'

From what those who knew her well have written or have spoken of, she clearly knew "a warmer kind of friendship" than passages such as those I have quoted suggest. I am sure this is so; it appears even in the few letters which have been published and in what Albertine Thévenon has written of her in the avant-propos to "La condition ouvrière," for instance.[12] There are also passages like that in:

"What did I care that there were other people to love? The love that I directed towards him, accompanied by outlines in my mind for exchanges of ideas which could only take place with him, was without an object" (*Notebooks*, Vol. I, p. 205).[13]

"Just as parents were unable to imagine that three years ago their child was non-existent, so we are unable to imagine a time when we did not know the beings we love" (p. 206).[14]

"I think I must love wrongly; otherwise things would not happen in this way to me" (p. 206).[15]

"To love in God is much more difficult than one thinks."[16]

I do not understand the sense of this 'I love wrongly' (J'aime mal). She is speaking here, as she often does, in a way I cannot grasp because my character is mediocre and shabby. I keep wanting to ask questions as though she had been using the words as I might have used them myself. I wonder why she says 'wrongly' (mal). "Si les choses . . . aimée de tout." (If things had not happened in this way . . . she would never have loved everything.)

This means that I do not understand the sense of 'love' in which God is said to love everyone or love the world: I do not understand the relation of this to that other sense in which we may speak of a deep love of a man for a woman or of a father for his son. When people tell me there is a *different* sense of love here, then I can follow, and I can follow also when they say that there are nevertheless important analogies. But Simone Weil wanted to go further than this, in some way; and so do most great religious writers.

If parents could make no difference between their love of their child and their love of anyone else, should we say that this showed a more perfect parental love? I remember a story by Flannery O'Connor (*The Lame Shall Enter First*) about a father who is so intent on helping children who are less fortunate than his own son, that it ends in tragedy for his son. (I think the author shows that he did not really love anyone.) Of course Simone Weil was familiar with considerations of this kind. I do not know what her answer would have been, and I do not think I could understand it anyway. If she felt compelled to say "I love wrongly" (j'aime mal) because her love was attached to certain others (attaché à quelques êtres) rather than being "open to everything that deserves to be loved" (disposible pour tout . . . aime), she would certainly have said that the attitude of the father was "worse" (pire): perhaps that he had not even got as far as "loving wrongly" (j'aime mal). She could see that

Christ's "Be perfect as your heavenly father is perfect" speaks of a move in a different direction—*away* from that of the father in the story. And I am sure that many people can understand her, as they understand the New Testament, with no trouble on this point. I do not understand the "comme votre père céleste" (as your heavenly father). I do not mention this because I think it is interesting to anyone, but only to explain my blindness and misunderstanding of much of what she says.

There is a passage further on in the same volume: "When a thing is perfectly beautiful, as soon as we fix our attention upon it, it represents unique and single beauty" (*Notebooks*, Vol. I, pp. 244–45).[17]

I think she means that if a human being is going to fix his attention on something—if he is to see it with his whole soul—then this must be *one* thing. "Those who are right don't regard all that which deserves to be loved with all their soul."[18] ("Ceux qui ont raison" evidently do *not* "regarder tout ce qui mérite d'être aimé de tout leur âme.")

Which should be said to love wrongly in this case? Or does each love wrongly in a different sense?

Here "the perfectly beautiful things" are, for example, Greek statues, the Catholic faith, Platonic thought, Hindu thought, and so forth. I do not know whether she would have said that her remark applied to love between human beings (e.g., man and woman, parents and children). Would she have said that to regard a human being with one's whole soul is in a sense more right than those who are right? I think she might. I am not sure. There are important differences, obviously.

Part of what she means by 'I love wrongly' (j'aime mal) is simply: "I'm a creature; I'm not God" (je suis une créature; ou: je ne suis pas Dieu). And we shall be misled if we confuse this sense of 'wrong' (mal) with that which distinguishes the love shown by one human being from that shown by another: these two men both love their sons, but this one loves wrongly (mais celui-ci aime mal, parce que), perhaps because his love was overloaded with pride and possessiveness, and so on. In this sense, when I love wrongly (quand j'aime mal), this is something of which I ought to be ashamed. But the other sense, of which I spoke just now, is that in which Simone Weil might also have said that my existence is an evil (mon existence est un mal), where this would have to be said of each individual saint as well as of each individual sinner. And although this is important in connexion with *humility* before God, it is not something of which I ought to be ashamed in the sense in which I ought to be ashamed of the cowardice or the pettiness I showed on this and that occasion.

NOTES

From a letter to M. O.'C. Drury dated 14 May 1962; Notes dated 5.6.62; From a letter to M. O.'C. Drury dated 24 May 1962; Notes dated 24.8.62; Notes dated 20.8.62; From a letter to Miss Miles dated 15 July 1964.

1. Rhees quotes from a longer paragraph that runs: "Beauty. A fruit one contemplates without stretching out one's hand. Also an affliction one contemplates without recoiling. The feeding of those that are hungry is a form of contemplation. In what way is it so?" *Notebooks* I, p. 283; French original: "Beauté: un fruit qu'on regarde sans tendre la main. De même un malheur qu'on regarde sans reculer. Nourrier ceux qui ont faim est une forme de contemplation. De quelle manière?" *Cahiers* II, p. 218.

2. "Aimer détaché. Supporter la pensée que ceux qu'on aime, à qui on pense avec amour, sont mortels, sont peut-être morts à l'instant même qu'on pense à eux. C'est une douleur. Ne jamais penser à un être humain, si on ne la pas à ses côtés, sans penser qu'il est peut-être mort." *Cahiers* II, p. 118.

3. Translation by Mario von der Ruhr and Timothy Tessin. "Exemple de prière.

Dire à Dieu:

Père, au nom du Christ, accorde-moi ceci.

Que je sois hors d'état de faire correspondre à aucune de mes volontés aucun mouvement du corps, aucune ébauche même de mouvement, comme un paralytique complet. Que je sois incapable de recevoir aucune sensation, comme quelqu'un qui serait complètement aveugle, sourd, et privé des trois autres sens. Que je sois hors d'état d'enchaîner par la moindre liaison deux pensées, même les plus simples, comme un de ces idiots complets qui non seulement ne savent ni compter ni lire, mais n'ont même jamais pu apprendre à parler. Que je sois insensible à toute espèce de douleur et de joie, et incapable d'aucun amour pour aucun être, pour aucune chose, ni même pour moi-même, comme les vieillards complètement gâteux.

Père, au nom du Christ, accorde-moi réellement tout cela.

Que ce corps se meuve ou s'immobilise, avec une souplesse ou une rigidité parfaites, en conformité ininterrompue avec ta volonté. Que cette ouïe, cette vue, ce goût, cet odorat, ce toucher, reçoivent l'empreinte parfaitement exacte de ta création. Que cette intelligence, dans la plénitude de la lucidité, enchaîne toutes les idées en conformité parfaite avec ta vérité. Que cette sensibilité éprouve dans leur plus grande intensité possible et dans toute leur pureté toutes les nuances de la douleur et de la joie. Que cet amour soit une flamme absolument dévorante d'amour de Dieu pour Dieu. Que tout cela soit arraché à moi, dévoré par Dieu, transformé en substance du Christ, et donné à manger à des malheureux dont le corps et l'âme manquent de toutes les espèces de nourriture. Et que moi, je sois un paralysé, aveugle, sourd, idiot et gâteux.

Père, opère cette transformation maintenant, au nom du Christ; et bien que je la demande avec une foi imparfaite, exauce cette demande comme si elle était prononcée avec une foi parfaite.

Père, puisque tu es le Bien et que je suis le médiocre, arrache de moi ce corps et cette âme pour en faire des choses à toi, et ne laisse subsister de moi, éternellement, que cet arrachement lui-même, ou bien le néant.

De telles paroles n'ont une vertu efficace que si elles sont dictées par l'Esprit. Ce n'est pas volontairement qu'on peut demander pareilles choses. C'est malgré soi qu'on en arrive là. Malgré soi, mais on y consent. On n'y consent pas avec abandon. On y consent avec une violence opérée par l'âme entière sur l'âme entière. Mais le consentement est entier et sans réserve, donné d'un mouvement unique de tout l'être.

Est-ce là que vient la métaphore du mariage? Ce rapport entre Dieu et l'âme ressemble à celui de l'époux avec l'épouse encore vierge, la nuit des noces. Le mariage est un viol consenti. Ainsi l'union de l'âme avec Dieu. L'âme a froid et ne sent pas qu'elle aime Dieu. Elle ne sait pas elle-même que si elle n'aimait pas elle ne consentirait pas. L'union conjugale se prépare, elle qui va faire de la personne d'un homme un simple intermédiaire entre sa chair et Dieu.

D'autres âmes aiment Dieu comme une femme aime son amant. Mais les amours des amants ne sont pas durables. Les époux seuls sont une seule chair pour toujours.

(Mais tous ces phénomènes spirituels sont absolument hors de ma compétence. Je n'y connais rien. Ils sont réservés à des êtres qui possèdent, pour commencer, les vertus morales élémentaires. J'en parle au hasard. Et je ne suis même pas capable de me dire sincèrement que j'en parle au hasard.)" Simone Weil, *La Connaissance Surnaturelle*, Paris: Gallimard, 1950, pp. 204–6.

4. Compare Jean Giraudoux, "Életre," in *Théatre Complet*, Paris: Gallimard, 1982, pp. 593–686.

5. *The Notebooks,* Vol. I, trans. by Arthur Wills, London: Routledge and Kegan Paul, 1956. The translation reads: "Whatever happens to me, how could I ever come to regard affliction as too heavy, since the wound of affliction and the abasement to which those whom it strikes are condemned opens to them the knowledge of human misery, knowledge which is the door, the passage leading to all wisdom?" (p. 236).

6. "We must be nothing in order to be in our true place in the whole" (p. 236).

7. ". . . that human misery represents a constant and irreducible quantity and exists in each man in the largest possible form; and that greatness comes from a one and only God, so that every man is identical with every other man" (p. 237).

8. "J'aime mal, il me semble, ou les choses ne se passeraient pas ainsi pour moi." Simone Weil, *Cahiers*, Vol. II, Paris: Librairie Plon, 1953, p. 99.

9. "Quant une chose est parfaitement belle, dès qu'on y fixe l'attention, elle est la seule beauté." *Cahiers*, Vol. II, pp. 159–60.

10. ". . . il y a la foi en un amour inconditionnel. C'est 'l'amour de ce qui n'existe pas', qui n'est pas à la merci de la mort, que ni les maladies ne peuvent défigurer, ni le caprice nous empêcher d'apprécier. S'il n'existe pas, c'est parce qu'en cette négation nous trouvons une sécurité qui manque à ce qui existe." Jacques Cabaud, *L'Expérience vécue de Simone Weil*, Paris: Librairie Plon, 1957, pp. 268–69.

11. "La vulnérabilité des choses précieuses est belle parce qu'elle est une marque d'existence. (. . .) Ainsi la vulnérabilité de l'âme au froid, à la faim. . . ." *Connaissance Surnaturelle*, p. 16.

12. Albertine Thévenon, Preface to Simone Weil, *La Condition Ouvrière*, Paris: Gallimard, 1951, pp. 11–12.

13. "Que m'importait qu'il y eût d'autres gens à aimer? L'amour que je dirigeais, vers lui, accompagné d'ébauches intérieurs d'échanges qui ne pouvaient avoir lieu qu'avec lui, était sans objet." *Cahiers* II, p. 98.

14. "Comme des parents ne peuvent se représenter qu'un enfant ait été néant trois ans auparavant, de même on ne peut se représenter qu'on n'ait pas toujours connu des êtres qu'on aime." Ibid., p. 99.

15. "J'aime mal, il une semble, ou les choses ne se passeraient pas ainsi pour moi." Ibid.

16. "Aimer en Dieu est bien plus difficile qu'on ne croit." Ibid.

17. "Quand une chose est parfaitement belle, dès qu'on y fixe l'attention, elle est la seule beauté." *Cahiers* II, pp. 159–60.

18. *Notebooks,* Vol. I, p. 245.

CHAPTER TEN

FRIENDSHIP AND PURITY OF SOUL

What does Simone Weil mean by 'purity'?

It is important in what she says about the love of God, and the distinction between the true love of God and idolatry.

Sometimes she uses it in contrast to 'base' or 'degraded', and this has analogies with its use in 'pure gold' or 'pure silver' in contrast to what is debased or adulterated. There is often a suggestion that what is adulterated or diluted is sham or counterfeit, while what is pure is the genuine article: there is a judgement of value here too.

In the first part of the *Phaedo* Socrates speaks of philosophy as purification: this is the purification of the soul from the contaminating influence of the body. But I think the important point is the *unification* of the soul. The senses and the bodily passions distract the soul by their multiplicity; they pull it this way and that, until it reels and wanders, hardly knowing where it is going. Plato emphasizes this notion of unification again in what he says of education in the *Republic*. The aim of education is to enable the pupil to become "one man and not many." This is the notion which Kierkegaard emphasizes in his *Purity of Heart*, where he takes as his text St. James's "Purify your hearts, ye double-minded." In the *Timaeus* Plato speaks of the existence of the forms as "indivisible existence" and of the existence of sensible and perishable things as "divisible existence."

When the *Phaedo* speaks of philosophy as purification, this is a Pythagorean idea, I think, and it is meant also in the sense of 'purification' in religion. I cannot understand this sense except vaguely. The notion of purification by sacrifice is connected with it—the purification by sprinkling the blood of goats and heifers, for instance. This is the origin of the present idea of 'absolution', I suppose. ("Go in peace." Compare what the *Phaedo* says of the distraction and the turmoil of the soul under the domination of the body.)

Simone Weil emphasizes the religious sense in Plato's dialogues. And she might have followed the notion of 'unity' in the *Republic*, at least in the sense that the unity and purity of the soul is a "harmony" of the soul. I have in mind the emphasis which she gives to the notion of harmony in her discussion of the Pythagoreans in *Intimations of Christianity*. She explains that the Pythagoreans often used 'harmony' as a synonym for 'logos' or for 'number': 'logos' generally meant ratio or proportion, in this connexion, but it also meant proof. But she is speaking of the way the Pythagoreans used this idea of proportion or of harmony to explain the relation of the world to God: the relation of what is never the same to what is always the same. And if she did speak of harmony in connexion with the human soul, I do not know whether she would have meant the harmony *within* the soul, to which the *Republic* speaks, or whether she would be thinking only of its relation to God. Probably she did think of purity of soul as some sort of harmony or order within the soul as well. Plato would also have said that the harmony or unity of the soul cannot be complete so long as it is the soul of a perishable body; it was a more or less perfect likeness of the unity or harmony which belongs to what is eternal.

This notion of *perfect* harmony or perfect unity is difficult, but it is connected with the notion of what is ideal in the sense in which mathematics is ideal. Wittgenstein used to speak of a direction in which our investigations are pushed, or of a direction in which we work in making our productions or our measurements more and more accurate. The wheel-wright or the turner on the lathe tries to make his productions more perfectly circular—or rejects them because they are too much out. The 'geometrical article' or the 'perfect circle': these are expressions which enter into our accounts of what we are doing with physical things, although it would have no sense to say that a physical thing *was* a geometrical circle—that it was exactly D-pi. And similarly with such expressions as 'perfectly straight line', 'perfectly equal', 'perfectly regular polygon', and so on, or geometrical straight line, geometrical equality.

This way of speaking *may* give rise to confusions, too, although it does not do so in the workshop. When the foreman throws out certain products as "rejects" or "seconds" or "imperfect," he does not mean that those he has passed are "perfect" in the sense of 'geometrical'. And it does not make sense to say that a very skilled worker has produced a perfect watch or a perfect wheel. If then someone were to say, "no one can ever produce a *perfectly* circular wheel," or "no one can produce a square frame which is *perfectly* square," this must not be taken to mean that every wheel or frame that is produced is imperfect. For if it did mean this, then the "no one *can* produce it" would mean it was *physically* impossible. To say that you cannot produce a geometrical circle does not mean this at all: it means that "This man has produced a geometrical circle" is nonsense. It is not as though we had an idea of a product which no one could make. And it is no *criticism* of what has been turned out to say that it is not geometrically perfect.

I imagine that Plato saw this. But I am less certain of his uses of 'perfect righteousness' and 'perfect beauty' or 'pure righteousness' and 'pure beauty'. Is there a sense in which you *could* say that a man had acted with perfect righteousness, analogous to that in which you might say that the workers in his factory had produced a perfect watch, or that the welder has made a perfect weld? The difficulty is that *criticism* does not quite mean the same in the two cases. Of course I may say, "I think he was entirely blameless in that affair," and I may mean this not simply in a negative sense; I may mean to say that I think his conduct throughout was admirable. But should I say also that I think he achieved perfect righteousness? I doubt if anyone would say this. And the reason might be that in this case anyway 'perfect' means 'divine'. And yet I think both Plato and Simone Weil did hold that in my criticism of *myself* or my judgement of myself I ought to measure myself by what is perfect, so that I have always to recognize that I have *fallen short*. Whereas if I were a lathe operator I should not measure the *excellence* of my achievement by a *geometrical* standard. In morality we seem to say, "There is always room for improvement," meaning that I have not done as well as I ought to have done.

Wittgenstein used to say that Plato confused the qualities of a thing with the ingredients of a mixture. If I say that this liquid is alcoholic or that it is oily, I mean that it has this or that ingredient. And perhaps it would have sense to say that *pure* alcohol is more alcoholic than any alcoholic drink. It may seem at times as though Plato were speaking of beauty as something to be found in beautiful things, and of pure beauty as more beautiful than any beautiful thing. If the presence of beauty in things can make them beautiful, then beauty itself must be dazzling. Of course the analogy limps because if alcohol is present in some liquid which is *not* alcoholic, it will make the whole mixture alcoholic, and if we were to say that beauty is present in something which is *not* beautiful—this will not do. And yet it seems as though Plato meant that the beauty is being limited or dulled by being mixed with what is not beautiful, just as alcohol is diluted and weakened by being mixed with what is not alcohol.

Plato might have said something similar of righteousness (of which the pure form might be holiness or divinity). Consider what Simone Weil says about "supernatural virtues"—of humility and of compassion, for instance. It is the presence of what is perfect in what is imperfect, what is pure in what is impure.

Simone Weil speaks of pure compassion and of impure, and also of pure friendship and of impure friendship.

Compassion:

> (I)t is certain that the strong will accomplish his purpose to the extreme limit of possibility. It is a mechanical necessity. Otherwise it would be as though he willed and did not will simultaneously. There is a necessity for the strong as well as the weak in this way. When two human beings have to settle something and neither has the power to impose anything on the other, they have to come to an understanding. (. . .) But when there is a strong and a weak, there is no need to unite their wills. There is only one will, that of the strong.[1]
>
> The supernatural virtue of justice consists of behaving exactly as though there were equality when one is the stronger in an unequal relationship. . . . Gratitude on the part of the unfortunate, when it is pure, is but a participation in this same virtue. (*Waiting on God*, pp. 100–1)[2]
>
> . . . it happens, although extremely rarely, that a man will forbear out of pure generosity to command where he has the power to do so. . . . The attention is creative . . . at least, if it is pure . . . Gratitude which is pure, like pure compassion, is essentially the acceptance of affliction . . . it recognizes (the Good) as the archetype of the secret point which lies at the centre of human personality and which is the principle of renunciation." (*Waiting on God*, pp. 101–5)[3]

Friendship:

There is however a personal and human love which is pure and which enshrines an intimation and a reflection of divine love . . .

When a human being is in any degree necessary to us, we cannot desire his good unless we cease to desire our own. Where there is necessity there is constraint and domination. . . . The most frequent cause of necessity in the bonds of affection is a combination of sympathy and habit . . .

A friendship is tarnished as soon as necessity triumphs, if only for a moment, over the desire to preserve the faculty of free consent on both sides. In all human things, necessity is the principle of impurity. All friendship is impure if even a trace of the wish to please, or the contrary desire to dominate is found in it. . . . Friendship is a miracle by which a person consents to view from a certain distance, and without coming any nearer, the very being who is as necessary to him as food. . . . (I)t has in it, at the same time as affection, something not unlike a complete indifference . . .

The simple fact of having pleasure in thinking in the same way as the beloved being—or in any case the fact of desiring such an agreement of opinion, attacks the purity of the friendship and at the same time as its intellectual integrity . . .

Pure friendship is an image of the original and perfect friendship which belongs to the Trinity and which is the very essence of God. (*Waiting on God*, pp. 152–60)[4]

I do not know the relation or the difference between God and the Father's love for the Son, and his love for the world. Is his love for the world an "image" of his love for the Son?

However that may be, Simone Weil's account of pure friendship is a caricature; and this is partly because she cannot conceive of its *purity* unless it is an image of the divine love—that love which shines like the sun on all equally and universally. This makes her veer away from treating friendship as something personal and so as *different* from compassion. She ends by treating it, at best, as indistinguishable from compassion.

She shows no conception of the difficulties which there are in friendship. And so she shows no appreciation of the nobility or the greatness which may appear in it.

One reason for this is her narrow—and I think arbitrary—view of the motives which men may have when they are acting "from necessity." She seems to be saying that when a man is acting from motives which arise in him in the natural course of events, then he *must* try to impose his will on another person. "This is a mechanical necessity." But this is making assumptions for which I can see no justification. (She admired Descartes and Spinoza. But at times she makes one think she would follow Descartes in holding that the life and behaviour of animals is purely mechanical: that animals are automata. I am sure she would not say this if she were challenged. But I am puzzled when she speaks of everything which she calls "bodily" or "animal" in human beings as moving from a "purely mechanical necessity" and then speaks as though when human relations are governed by bodily or animal desires, they must be decided by the movement of what has greater mass and the greater momentum. The stronger always exercises his will to the limit, and his will is always to override and subdue. But this is not true of animals, even if it were generally true of "mechanical necessity.")

When people distinguish between bodily desires and motives of the spirit, it is often hard to see why the line is drawn just where it is. I suppose everyone would agree that there is an important distinction between "higher" and "lower" interests in human beings, although people do not agree on how this distinction should be described, and they may differ in details—sometimes important ones—regarding what should be ranked as higher and what as lower. One may speak vaguely of the difference between two sorts of life which a man may live: a life devoted to material gain or personal advancement, the securing of bodily comforts and enjoyment of coarser pleasures, or a life devoted to interests which are "disinterested" in the sense at least that they do not bring material gain or advancement or bodily comforts, such as art, science, friendship, and religion. This may be called either being concerned with things of the body or being concerned with things of the soul, and some people (I am thinking of Renan) have said that this is the sense of the distinction between soul and body, a distinction which is confused when people speak of different substances. Well, I can follow this to a considerable extent, but already we have run into an element of fiction, and it is hard to know just how to take it. I say "fiction," because I do not know that Renan wanted to suggest that anyone ever does lead *purely* the one sort of life or purely the other, in fact the distinction of soul and body, and so the distinction between the two lives, would be found in every human being. It is not as though he had made his distinction clearer by pointing to actual examples which we can all recognize—as though he had pointed to two historical characters and said "someone like this" and "someone like that"—so that by looking at the examples we could fill in the blanks. We still do not know how to fill in the blanks. And above all, we do not know how the two brief lists are related to one another—how 'soul' and 'body' are related to one another—since they are not related as the different lives of different individuals might be.

Neither does it help if you point first to the lives of human beings and then to the lives of animals. Suppose someone (say Aristotle) asked first how human beings *differed* from animals, and then said that this difference gives you what we mean by the human soul. Well, what is the human body then? This differs from animal bodies, and it includes much, at least, of what distinguishes human beings from animals, which was supposed to show what belongs to the human *soul*. For we are speaking of a living body, not a corpse; just as we were speaking of a living soul and not a ghost. ("Descartes," said Professor Kemp Smith, "imagined that a human being was a mysterious union of a corpse and a ghost.") And if we say that someone seems concerned only to satisfy his bodily needs and desires, we do not mean that any animal has ever lived in the way he does.

So I do not think the adjective 'animal' helps much. If we want to distinguish between what is sacred in human life and what is not, we cannot describe "what is not sacred" ("material desires" as opposed to "spiritual" ones) as whatever human life has in common with the lives of animals.

When Aristotle suggested the definition of man as "a biped animal capable of discourse," he was fastening on what I think is the most important thing. All that we may call the refinement of human desires and capacities towards spirituality—the refinement of love, for instance—is connected with the use of language, and it would not have been possible without it. I wish Simone Weil might have paid more attention to this. On the other hand, it is also the role of language in their lives which has made possible the baseness and degradation of human beings, which also distinguishes them from animals. I *think* one can say that if this sort of development (towards degradation) had not been possible, the other (towards spirituality) would not have been possible either.

The distinction between soul and body seems to me largely a moral distinction. But just for that reason I do not find it helpful to speak of it as a distinction between what operates from mechanical necessity and what does not, or between what moves according to gravity and what does not.

I cannot make anything of the suggestion that in base actions and in noble actions human beings move according to different laws—as though the difference between base and noble could be described in this way. I do not see how one can sensibly compare "the laws of gravitation" and "the laws of grace"—as though this were like comparing the laws of dynamics and the laws of statics, or the laws of hydraulics and the laws of optics.

Simone Weil often follows Plato, and she speaks sometimes as though she were taking over the term 'necessity' from him. But she transforms the idea into something he would not have admitted. For Plato 'necessity' was always contrasted with 'reason'; "what happens of necessity" was never something which could be studied and understood in science. The movements of the stars and all that was studied in astronomy was *contrasted* with what happens of necessity, and Plato would have said the same of the subject matter of the physics of Galileo and Newton. But Simone Weil seems to think of necessity first and foremost as what is described in Newtonian physics. Plato speaks of the influence of political life—the obsession with prestige and with "success"—as the operation of necessity. Simone Weil wants to call this necessity too, and she refers to Plato, but she seems also to speak of it as a *mechanical* necessity in the Newtonian sense, and Plato would certainly not have agreed to this. He did *not* mean a necessity that can be expressed in any law and made a subject of calculations. I wish I knew whether Simone Weil *does* mean this when she is talking of human actions. She often *seems* to. But she *may* intend only a metaphor. In any case it is not clear.

In his account of friendship, I do not think Plato is very much better than Simone Weil. I am thinking, for instance, of the way the *Symposium* speaks of a transition from the love of a particular person to the love of all beautiful people and the love of the beautiful or just institutions—as though this were the development or the flowering of what had appeared as love of that one person. It is true, of course, that being in love with someone may *awaken* a man to the beauty of other people and the beauty of nature, and perhaps to a sense of justice in political institutions: the idea of a noble life and what makes this possible. But Plato speaks there as though the love of that person were itself *transferred* to the love of these more general matters, so that the person I first loved no longer counts in my life any more than the many beautiful people and beautiful things in nature do. Perhaps I am misunderstanding Plato, and I hope I may be.

Plato emphasizes the connexion between love and the recognition of beauty. And the way he thinks of this—the connexion between love and beauty—is what drives him that way, I think. Beauty "acts" with the sort of universality which God's love has, it inspires a love of anything it reaches or enters into. Plato can then speak of a "purification" of love through my efforts to find the true beauty which the person I love has partially revealed to me. But in this case, as my love does become more pure, it ceases to be personal love and ceases to be friendship.

I *think* he would hold also that my love can never be quite pure as long as I am compelled to take account of particular things at all, that is, never in this life.

But how does this help us? If I say of two people that the purity of their friendship has suffered, or that something has destroyed the purity of their friendship, am I using the expression in such a way that it would make no *sense* to say that pure friendship had ever been found? Clearly not, for I have just said that it has been lost.

I will not say there is just no sense in speaking of an "ideal case" in connexion with friendship. But I do not see clearly what the sense would be. And it clearly cannot have much analogy to the sense in which we may speak of an "ideal circle" or "geometrical circle." For we can give a clear account of this expression in geometry and we cannot give any such clear account of "ideal friendship" or "ideally pure friendship."

Simone Weil sometimes speaks of the love of what is pure as a love of what does not exist—just as the love of what is "ideal" is a love of what does not exist. At other times she insists that "pure generosity," for instance, does sometimes occur. I do not know what distinguishes the one sense of 'pure' from the other in her writings.

In general, though, when she speaks of pure generosity, pure compassion, pure attention, she is not exactly *describing* what happens. It is a way of estimating or *judging* what has happened.

Nor is it a description of what happens when she says, "It is not we who show the compassion, but God in us." And I partly understand this. But . . . what kind of mistake should I be making if I said it *was* the man himself who showed the compassion? Or is it nonsense to ask this?

Obviously there is no way of looking to find out whether it is he or God acting through him.

It is no help to refer to "a feeling of being impelled." For one thing, such a feeling by itself would not show that the impulsion did not come from the devil.

Perhaps Simone Weil would want to say that I may show compassion "against my will." But we might wish to have this more precisely described, since someone might ask whether that did not show that the compassion was not genuine.

The point is that I do not think the alternative is rightly put in that way: "Was it I, or was someone doing it for me?" If I try to lift a heavy weight, I may be surprised to find that I am lifting it so easily, and then I find that someone behind my back (or without my seeing him) was assisting me by lifting as well. There can be nothing of this sort in the present case. It is not that I am surprised to find that I show compassion after all and then discover that it was really God.

"If it was *not* I showing compassion, then God was not showing compassion through *me*, however he might show it in other ways."

Why should not God show compassion for certain people by making me show hatred towards them, or behave cruelly towards them? Would not Simone Weil say that God showed compassion for Jesus by allowing him to be crucified? "It was not Judas who betrayed Jesus, it was God acting through him." That the scriptures might be fulfilled. Also with Caiaphas.

Why should I not say that God is showing compassion through me no matter what I do? And then why say that it is not I who shows the compassion when I do show compassion?

It might be said that it is only after much prayer and thought of God that I do show compassion, and that my showing it is an answer to prayer. But I do not think Simone Weil means just this. In the first place, when she is speaking of the implicit love of God, she says that some show compassion when they have not prayed (or at least have not known that they were praying). And in any case I think she wants to say that there is something about the act of compassion itself which is divine.

The difficulty is in the statement that if it is divine, it is not my act. Perhaps this is said because of some idea of original sin. Perhaps it is because it would be pride if I said that it was divine and *was* my act.

On the other hand, when the afflicted person feels pure gratitude, he feels it towards the *man* who has shown compassion. This is what gives the special character to the whole transaction.

The man might say that it is only by realizing that the act did not come from him that he *can* recognize it as divine. This would be his reason for saying that it was God acting through him. He does not know how he was able to achieve any such act of compassion. He recognizes too much in himself—vanity, especially—which would have prevented it. The charity which he has shown seems to be independent of everything which he feels as belonging to himself. So it need not be that he "feels someone else is helping him." What he does feel is that the act did not come from him. This is not because it "happened automatically," as my arm rises when I have been pressing it against the wall. He might say it was *impossible* for him to recognize that as an act of compassion and not be sure that it came from some other spirit than his own.

I do not think this covers the case of a person who shows compassion and does not believe in God. In this case the man himself would have no sense of the act as divine, and it is not clear that he would feel like saying that it did not come from him. Perhaps this sort of question just never occurred to him.

Weil regards certain motives as supernatural because they *could* not be natural; natural influences and forces all tend in one direction. "You cannot explain a generous act by reference to the laws of mechanics." But will the laws of mechanics explain an envious or a jealous action either? The "explanation" would presumably lie in showing that such an action could have been predicted by anyone who knew these and these conditions. And here the trouble is partly just that Simone Weil does recognize the occurrence of generosity and other supernatural actions—actions which could not have been predicted. But if they could not have been predicted, then neither could I have predicted that they would *not* occur. And for this reason I cannot predict with anything like the certainty of mechanics that a selfish or self-assertive action would occur. In this case, how can we say that the self-assertive action can be accounted for by mechanics or by gravity? The trouble is that we do not know when gravity is going to operate and when it is not.

What is important is that God *reveals* himself in the act of compassion—in a manner analogous to that in which he is revealed in natural beauty. And in so far as the recipient does recognize the beauty of the act of justice or compassion, he does recognize the divinity of it.

It is not in *this* way that God reveals himself through evil. You cannot explain shockingly selfish actions on the *general* principle that men are by nature selfish, because the really shockingly selfish or evil actions are not the general rule.

Why should we say that the vilest actions are any more "natural" than the purest compassion is?

Simone Weil's notions of 'the supernatural' and of God the Father 'who art in heaven' seems to be bound up with a notion of a purity which does not "exist." I have not tried to explain this. I have only tried to say why I find it hard to understand.

NOTES

From Notes dated 29.4.63.

1. *Waiting on God*, p. 99: "Si on la suppose connue, il est certain que le fort accomplira sa volonté jusqu'à l'extrême limite de la possibilité. C'est une nécessité mécanique. Autrement, ce serait comme s'il voulait et ne voulait pas en même temps. Il y a la nécessité pour le fort comme pour le faible. Quand deux êtres humains ont à faire ensemble, et qu'aucun n'a le pouvoir de rien imposer à l'autre, il faut qu'ils s'entendent. (. . .) Mais quand il y a un fort et un faible il n'y a nul besoin d'unir deux volontés. Il n'y a qu'une volonté, celle du fort." *Attente de Dieu*, p. 103.

2. "La vertu surnaturelle de justice consiste, si on est le supérieur dans le rapport inégal des forces, à se conduire exactement comme s'il y avait égalité. . . . La reconnaissance chez le malheureux, quand elle est pure, n'est qu'une participation à cette même vertu." Simone Weil, *Attente de Dieu*, Paris: La Colombe, nd, pp. 104–5.

3. ". . . il arrive, quoique ce soit extrêmement rare, que par pure générosité un homme s'abstienne de commander là où il en a le pouvoir. . . . Cette attention est créatrice . . . du moins si elle est pure. . . . La gratitude pure comme la compassion pure est essentiellement consentement au malheur. . . . Elle reconnaît le bien comme le modèle du point secret qui se trouve au centre de la personne humaine et qui est le principe de renoncement." Ibid., pp. 104–9.

4. "L'amitié pure est une image de l'amitié—originelle et parfaite qui est celle de la Trinité et qui est l'essence même de Dieu." *Attente de Dieu*, p. 161.

CHAPTER ELEVEN

THE TEMPORAL AND THE ETERNAL

OBEDIENCE

"All true friendship is mediated by Christ."[1] What sort of proposition is that? giving something of the meaning of true friendship (amité vraie)?

When Simone Weil speaks of that part of the soul which is eternal (cette partie de l'âme qu'est éternelle), she must be thinking of what she refers to in "Human Personality."[2] (Certainly not what Aristotle called the intellectual part.) That which can cry "Why am I being harmed?" (Pourquoi fait on moi de mal?) That 'Why' (pourquoi) which is a sense of living at a distance from God, and at the same time before God. The main point is that it is not a question about the operation of la pesanteur. Nakedness of soul; of spirit (nudité de l'âme et de l'esprit). "Neither talking nor thinking about God; not uttering this word except when one cannot do otherwise." ('Cannot' here evidently has a particular sense.)[3] "It is not the 'peut' of the realm of force or necessity. The cry that comes from the soul. That to which is addressed the 'Quel est ton tourment?'"

The reason why affliction is evidence of the tenderness of God: since it makes one aware of the misère which is human existence. Makes—quickens—that which may cry pourquoi? The same would be true of compassion, provided this be genuine, and not for the sake of prestige. For the sake of prestige—(cf. Father Sergius)—with the attempt to relieve or console the suffering for which one feels compassion. The tenderness of God is giving the constant 'vide' which must be borne without consolation. And this is the love of God. The misery or misfortune of those in whom the 'vide' is filled by the "shadows" or satisfactions of the world of the Great Beast. The important connexion or identification of 'la sacre' and justice.

That the "part éternelle" was not her talent or her intelligence is plain from the letter in which she speaks of the transitoriness of this, and of its subjection to the world of necessity. Her need to discover whether there was *anything* in her which would *not* be taken away by force, in this way. This was the most important question to be asked. And to know that was to know la vérité as far as may be. It is to know—or to have some sense—of the relation of the temporal to the eternal. The relation of what is "corruptible"—what is subject to force—and what is not.

If you pronounce the name of God under other circumstances, on this occasion or from other interests, then you pronounce it from motives other than the love of God. And this is idolatry, something which raises a "screen," and makes the love of God all but impossible. Similarly with thanking God for blessings which come through the order of necessity. Thanking him for good fortune. All of this is a form of turning away from God.[4]

Simone Weil wanted to look on "necessity"—events happening according to laws—as "perfect obedience": obedience to the will of God. She distinguished between following necessity (which would be submission to the will of God), and submission to force, since she held that in the happening according to necessity force is not the last or final governor. I think there is something important here; although it is not easy to become clear about it.

But she does seem to make obedience a matter of complete *passivity*, even if it is not merely submission to force. And I imagine that some of what she says about the elimination of the person is connected with this. It is also part of her view that attention is more important than "volonté."

On the other hand, if she *is* saying that "perfect" or "absolute" obedience is also perfect passivity, then I would think she is wrong. She would be making some sort of distinction between willing obedience and acting because one is overcome by force majeure. But I should have thought that *willing* obedience were something more positive than she allows.

Suppose she were to speak of something which I do as falling short of perfect obedience. What is it that would keep it from being perfect? Or should we ask: "What is there about my action which is really disobedience?" Presumably we should have here a case of what she would call "impurity"; this would generally be the attempt to satisfy personal desires. I do not see how she can speak of obedience or of disobedience at all if she *does* eliminate "the personal."

I do not remember her discussing "disobedience." But neither do I remember her discussing the distinction between 'voluntary' and 'involuntary'. (If I give an uninhibited sneeze, why is this not an example of perfect obedience to the will of God?) And this distinction is probably the more fundamental one. There is something wrong—or to say the least, confusing—in speaking of my involuntary movements as being acts of perfect obedience. But in the same way, of course, it were queer (wrong, I think) to speak of the movements of the waves and falling stones as perfect obedience. She does so because she wants to insist that the persistence of any force is always *limited*: that it operates in submission to a "limit" or "equilibrium." And she does not want to say that this restriction itself is imposed by force, since that would clearly be absurd. It is a restriction of another sort, and she wants therefore to speak of *submission* of another sort. Her argument seems to be: since the submission is itself not the operation of any force, it must be the operation of love. And this is the reason for speaking of it as obedience.

A great deal of her discussion of *evil* and of *affliction* is connected with this. Evil is always in some sense subjective, and in this way illusory. "They know not what they do."

Whatever happens, happens in accordance with the will of God. Whatever happens, happens in *obedience,* or *is* obedience, to the will of God. Our difficulty here is partly that of understanding the notion of 'the will of God' at all. I can speak of what is done in obedience to the will of a boss. "He is doing that because he has been told to." I can speak of someone as *trying* to do the will of his father or of his loved one. But in all these cases the notion is tolerably clear because we can sensibly ask, "As opposed to what?" I should be able to say something about the difference between acting in obedience to someone's will, and acting not in obedience to someone's will. Similarly, I can say something of the distinction between voluntary and involuntary actions: between movements which I make because I want to make them, and movements in which I am thrown or pushed, for instance. And in speaking of the will of God, the difficulty is in saying that "*whatever* happens happens in obedience to the will of God." If that be so, then we do not seem to be saying anything *about* what happens; and yet I think that Simone Weil thought that she was.

It may be that this is something characteristic of religious statements about the world. And the mistake would be in thinking of these as a continuation of statements of matters of fact. She is not ascribing a character to happenings or to things in the sense she would be if she were to say, "This stone is brittle," which would tell you something about it, because for all you knew it might have been a stone which was not brittle.

She would still say that "Whatever happens, happens in obedience to the will of God" is not empty. She might even say that in *one* sense it is the expression of a discovery which she has made about things, although of course it were nonsense to take this in the sense in which one speaks of making a discovery in natural science.

"That is how things are. That is how they should be viewed. That is how you will see things if you understand them." And if we asked, "By what criterion do you distinguish the way in which things should be viewed from ways in which they should not be viewed? What decides for you that this *is* the way in which they should be viewed?"—I think she would have an answer, although it would be unlike an answer to questions about matters of fact, and although she might think there was something stupid in the way you asked the question.

One of the important notions is that of 'understanding things', where this does not mean understanding this or that particular sort of thing or particular sort of happening.

TIME AND FREEDOM

"Time, strictly speaking, does not exist (except the present, as a limit), and yet it is that to which we are subjected" (*Notebooks*, Vol. I, p. 71).[5]

Much is confusing here, such as the 'pourtant': as though it were like saying "We are subjected to some pressure which does not exist," where we should know what were meant by saying that the pressure *did* exist.

'Subjected to time.' One might speak of being subjected to a particular curriculum, or a particular routine. We have no choice but to follow the various steps as they come. But this has sense because we could say what it were like if we were *not* subjected to the routine. And where one speaks of being "subjected to time," we do not know what being "freed from time" would be, and consequently it is hard to see what the sense of 'subjection' is here. (I wonder whether she is confusing 'time' with 'generation and decay' or 'coming to be and passing away'.)

No doubt Weil is thinking of the distinction of 'the temporal' and 'the eternal'. But the idea of time as "controlling" us or dominating us can hardly make sense, since these notions of 'control' or 'domination' are themselves temporal: control is exercised in time, and therefore it makes no sense to speak of time as controlling anything.

But in what way *is* matter "subject to time"? Almost as though time were something from whose properties we could deduce the second law of thermodynamics.

References to factory labour: "To work—if one is worn out—means becoming subjected to time in the same way as matter is. The mind is compelled to jump from one instant to the next. That is what constitutes obedience" (*Notebooks*, Vol. I, p. 79).[6] The suggestion that labour makes the workers aware of time and aware that they are *subject* to time. "He who has to labour every day feels in his body that time is inexorable" (*Notebooks*, Vol. I, p. 79).[7]

Compare: "The feeling we have is that the present disappears into the past without our being able to prevent it. And here we are obviously using the picture of a film strip remorselessly moving past us, that we are unable to stop. But it is of course just as clear that the picture is misapplied: that we cannot say 'Time flows' if by time we mean the possibility of change" (Rush Rhees, ed., *Ludwig Wittgenstein: Philosophical Remarks*, Oxford: Blackwell, 1964, §52, p. 83).[8]

Simone Weil contrasts the "blind" or mechanical operation with signs in certain parts of higher algebra, where there is no meaning even to *asking* what these signs signify, with what she calls "la pensée méthodique." She compares the algebraic work with carrying out a job in connexion with a machine: and she says of this that it is not, properly speaking, methodical, but that it conforms to—is performed according to—a method.

When she says that an understanding or knowledge of what is possible and what is impossible allows a man to free himself from the blind domination of the passions, she is speaking as Spinoza did. But it is also similar to her later insistence on *waiting* on God—when the grace, if it be constantly desired, will come of itself.

Freeing oneself from illusions (regarding what is possible and what is not) and from imagination. The idea that there is no such thing as a spiritual *force* (which might operate against the physical or material forces).

But it is surely wrong to say that an entirely free life would be one in which all real difficulties presented themselves (appeared as) problems of the sort met in geometry and arithmetic, in which all victories were like solutions put into action: "A completely free life would be one wherein all real difficulties presented themselves as kinds of problems, wherein all successes were as solutions carried into action" (*Oppression and Liberty*, p. 86).[9] In mathematics we always know what sort of thing a solution would be. And in this sense we know the "end" we are trying to achieve. The greatest difficulties in people's lives come where it is not like this. In a measure she recognizes this.

But later, when she is contrasting la personne et le sacré, she speaks of mathematical activity as 'anonyme'; and she seems to think of manual labour, when it is guided simply by the consideration of nécessité, in the same way.

In both cases, she is taking 'solution of problems' as the paradigm of coming to a decision: in fact the ideal case, the case of free action, in which there is nothing to decide: in which it is only a question of "pensée méthodique" in connexion with the given elements (éléments donnés).

"If you can see *why* you do what you do, if what you do follows from your own judgement in view of the éléments donnés, you are free."

This is her account of *pure* activity (of decision, 'pure' in the sense in which geometry is pure). "It is not possible to conceive of a nobler destiny for man than that which brings him directly to grips with naked necessity, without his being able to expect anything except through his own exertions, and such that his life is a continual creation of himself by himself" (*Oppression and Liberty*, p. 87).[10]

It is the phrase 'sans qu'il ait rien à attendre que de soi' (without being able to expect anything except through his own exertions) which is queer. And it is extremely important that she later spoke of this same sort of thing as *anonyme* (anonymous).

I agree that in much—perhaps most—of what I should call free activity, what is important about the work accomplished, the solution of a mathematical problem, for instance, is not that it has been performed by me. And probably much the same is true of artistic work; what she says about this is important.

"Creating the material conditions of one's own life" is somewhat difficult, as it really is in her account as well. And where it comes to "solving problems" in one's relation to other people, then it is hard to see anything of the sort. The thought of how someone else might have solved them—in what sense is this relevant? *Not at all* in the deep problems in marriage, for instance (of which she seems pretty oblivious). It is not relevant, except in a limited way, to the work of teaching either. And while I agree that the greatness of *Lear* may be called anonyme, it would mean nothing to say that it had been produced by la pensée méthodique from éléments donnés, although admittedly he was not dependent on anyone else's orders.

Weil thinks the relation of thought and the solution of a problem presents no difficulty when the pensée is really méthodique. Let us say that this is an internal relation. And if we could arrange a physical action as we can arrange the steps in the "methodical" solution of a problem, then the relation of thought to this physical action would offer no difficulty either: a problem in pure mechanics, so to speak.

But she sees a difficulty in the relation of the "action of thought" to the movements of my own body: "The immediate relationship linking our thoughts to our movements will always remain wrapped in impenetrable obscurity" (*Oppression and Liberty*, p. 89).[11] This seems a misconception of the problem about the relation of thought and action. Her trouble: We cannot treat bodily movement as presenting us with problems in pure mechanics. "At times the reactions of the living body are completely foreign to the mind" (*Oppression and Liberty*, p. 89).[12] (As if the internal relation would depend on thoughts *penetrating* the action, or having insight into this necessity.) As though it would be intelligible if bodily operations *were* mental operations.

The relation of thought and action as relation of thought and application (cf. a command and carrying out a command): this is very limited. This leaves out 'I' and so it does not touch my problems.

Consider her example, or her comparison, of the pilot guiding the ship by knowing how to control the forces of necessity through the rudder and through adjusting himself to the winds and so forth. Weil does not consider the difference between reason and motive and cause. When she speaks of reasons, it seems as though she thought only of proof. As though other sorts of reasons were given only faute de mieux, and under ideal conditions we should give only proof. A reason for acting seems to be a reason for taking this or that procedure, like the pilot guiding the ship. This is not what we most commonly mean by a reason for doing this or that, or by being faced with an alternative or a choice. Knowing what to do, for her, is knowing what factors are involved, and what would be necessary, what would be needed to meet them. Contrast Kierkegaard in *Der Begriff der Angst*, for instance.

The whole question of "the void" seems to be connected with this. I think it means that she is misconceiving the nature of humility and also the nature of what she calls pure love. Here again contrast Kierkegaard in *Purity of Heart*.

". . . without his being able to expect anything except through his own exertions, and such that his life is a continual creation of himself by himself" (*Oppression and Liberty*, p. 87).[13]

Here 'by himself' means 'by his thought'. And she seems almost to be defining 'la pensée', by reference to the solution of mathematical problems. In solving a mathematical problem I may appeal to someone else for help, or I may ask him to confirm or check what I have done: "Have I got it right?" The same would apply to a problem in engineering. Certainly you may say that I cannot perform a calculation without seeing myself that this follows. But ex hypothesi, I am not *responsible* for the conclusion. And for this reason I do not enter into it as I do in deciding to do something: for here it is *not* a performance that another could have done. The mathematical conclusion is not "mine" in the sense that my action is. What makes the action mine is not that I have an insight into the necessity of the conclusion. There may be nothing *at all* like that. Nor is it simply that I depend on my own judgement: I may do that in criticizing the action of someone else.

In fact there may be a difficulty about decisions—just in connexion with the fact that they are either made for certain reasons or at any rate can be *discussed* in terms of reasons for or against them. I have said that "I" would not enter otherwise. Compare Kant's conception of 'the rational will'. "Actions which follow from principles." On the other hand, if a decision is just carrying out a certain piece of reasoning, then I could have got it from someone else. Aristotle and the practical syllogism. I expect Plato would have called this sophistry. The art of reaching the true conclusion. Especially in connexion with politics. Sophistry as counterfeit politics, where politics is taken as the art of making men better. Contrast Socrates' method of catharsis, which may be what Simone Weil *thinks* she is describing.

Self-confrontation. Seeing the difference between what is genuine and what is illusion—between a life that is "awake" and one that is a lie. There seems to be nothing of this in Aristotle. And certainly there can be no formal account of how such a decision is made: not by a practical syllogism. Small wonder that Aristotle saw the chief difficulty in the form of akrasia. "Anybody can see what the right conclusion *is*. The difficulty is in carrying it out." I feel certain this is irrelevant to what Socrates was doing and saying.

What Simone Weil calls "attente" is not always quite the same as "attention," although it is frequently allied to it. She commonly has in mind the Greek word which was translated in Latin as 'patientia' (cf. 'possess one's soul in patience'), but for her it is closely connected with *desire*, at least when one is speaking of desire for the good; I am not sure that what she calls "bodily desire" is quite the same. And it is closely connected with prayer. And with humility. She says that such "attente"—or "prayer" or "patience"—may move God to come to one (she says something like "constrain God to come") "because it is the extreme of passivity." (Do not go seeking God. Do not try to find God who is hidden. *Cry* to God—that is all.)

"Attente" is connected with attention—or *is* attention—only in mystical experience. In fact it seems as though she were saying both that "attente" is the patience or refusal to try to find God—and hence the need for the extreme asceticism, the refusal to follow any kind of "seeking" which would be a form of idolatry—and also that "attente" is the way of reaching the mystical experience and of finding God.

But there are difficulties connected with this. I had been interested in the relation between "attention" and will (volonté) in her discussions. She sometimes speaks as though will were a stupefied effort to accomplish what were better left to patience and attention. "A strong will," she says, "can accomplish a great deal. As in Napoleon. A great deal— but not of what is good. Not even an atom of good."

In the *Notebooks* Weil speaks of attention in connexion with the direction of "spiritual énergie," and with the "liberation of énergie which is attached" to the satisfaction of desire. She asks how this liberation is to be accomplished. And she says:

> We have to desire that it should happen in us. Desire it truly. Simply desire it, and not try to achieve it yourself. Or even give your thought to it. For any attempt in that direction is vain and you pay dearly for it. In any undertaking of this sort everything called 'I' must be entirely passive. Attention alone—that attention which is so full that the 'I' vanishes—is what is required of me. Keep the light of attention away from everything called 'I' and turn it towards what is inconceivable.

Again: The effort of will towards virtue and the fulfilment of oblig-
ations has no value in itself, but only as a prayer without words, a
prayer by gestures, dumb.

There is much in the distinctions she is making in such passages
which I can understand. But she seems to think that "attention" may
achieve an *elimination* of the will. And I do not think this was so, even
in herself, not because the task was too much for her, but because there
is a contradiction, and it is a false task.

Of course, if 'exercise of my own will' means 'self-assertiveness',
then the case is clear enough. But she wants it to include more than this,
I think.

As a result, Weil lumps together what should be distinguished. And
she is unable to take account of much which is important—much that
you cannot discuss unless you recognize a distinction both between will
and attention and also between will and desire. "Doing the will of God"
generally includes "consent," or it often does, and she speaks of this
quite often. But you cannot go very far if you identify 'consent' either
with 'attention' or with 'pure passivity'.

BEAUTY

I have understood from her writings what is meant by thanks to God for
a realization that one's own existence has no worth, and in this connexion what it means to speak of feeling *equal* gratitude for joy and for
affliction. I have not found this understanding in any other religious
writer—St. Paul, St. Augustine, or Kierkegaard, for instance.

Without the realization of one's own worthlessness, there can be no
full appreciation of beauty: of the wonder of God, or the wonder or
nobility of the lives of the saints or other great men. No doubt this statement, as I have given it, is faulty and could be challenged. But I think
she has something important here. (In her account this is connected with
the rejection or opposition to "imagination," as a source of "mensonge." The *bonds* of the prisoners in the cave, that is, in the world, are
the imagination, preventing one from reaching true vision.)

This is connected with her idea of purity: nota bene, the pure lover
of God, as distinct from idolatry, of which she would say that it always
includes an idea that the satisfaction of one's personal desires or needs
is important.

She would say also that it is the precondition of being able to *learn* from what you contemplate—that you do not consider its effect upon you, "what it does for you," and so on. ("What you get out of it." In her view, this was Plato's teaching in the *Republic*.)

And yet one may feel that this view ("denying myself," "denying that I have any worth") is important in certain contexts—religious contemplation—and not in others. There are difficulties if you try to give a general account of *humility* in this way.

The humility of Christ, for instance; not to be denied. But in what sense could he have believed that his own existence was without value? "Why call ye me good?" and so forth. But also: "I am the vine and you are the branches."

(To speak of the humility of God would seem to me to have no sense at all. It would have no more sense to say that God has a sense of his own importance. Or so it seems to me. I do not understand 'God loves himself' or 'God can love only himself'. This is bringing in traits of *human* love which are out of place here. Just as 'a sense of one's own importance' is an expression that has sense when said of human beings, especially in their comparisons with one another.)

When Simone Weil says that the music of Bach and of Monteverdi could not have been written by anyone who had not himself led a holy life, she seems to be arguing largely that an evil tree cannot bring forth good fruit. Perhaps she would say it is not so very different when someone says that the special or divine character of Jesus can be seen in his sayings. I have been wont myself to say that the First Symphony of Schumann, for instance, could not have been written by anyone capable of great meanness (or perhaps of any sort of meanness). I do not think there need be anything wrong in this sort of judgement, although it is one which can be used carelessly.

One is inclined, in a similar way, to say that the work of Newton or of Galileo or of Archimedes could not have been written by anyone who was interested primarily in his own enjoyments. This is because the work is plainly of a kind demanding concentration which must disregard the appeal to what is normally called enjoyment. I expect that empirical investigation would bear this out. Perhaps especially that no work of this kind is possible with "doublemindedness."

But apart from this, it is not clear just what would be the mark of a *want* of chastity in her view. I think the Church holds specific actions— intercourse outside wedlock, "indecent touches," masturbation, and also attention to indecent literature or pictures (impure thoughts)—as acts of impurity, and as violations of chastity (or would the Church not say this latter?). I do not think Simone Weil would regard the *abstaining* from such actions as *sufficient* for chastity. I am more puzzled to know how strictly she would have thought this *necessary*.

Her emphasis is much more upon humility and compassion. It is for this reason that she can speak of Villon as having the character of a saint, in spite of his having committed thefts, and (although she does not mention this) in spite, perhaps, of his having "lived in sin." This brings in the conception of marriage as a sacrament—and of all intercourse as sinful which has not been sanctified in some way by the sacrament of marriage. I do not know what she has to say about this particular sacrament. On the other hand, the *purity* to which she became devoted when viewing the landscape from the mountain, did have some positive value—it was not important merely because humility and compassion are impossible without it. In the same way, chastity has often been connected with holiness—not in the sense of a necessary regimen, but because nothing like holiness could be without it.

Simone Weil would have connected the idea of chastity with that of 'nudity of spirit', and with the nudity of style which she sought and admired in writing; just as it would be connected with chastity or simplicity of style in music—especially the Gregorian chants—and in Romanesque architecture.

In all these there is what we might call exclusion of everything except the matter in hand (cf. "ne penser pas à . . . ," not thinking of . . .). In all the style excludes any striving after "effect." It is free from ornamentation and from gesturing—or from anything done in the hope of impressing one's readers or hearers. Impressive ornamentation takes the attention away from what is being said or done, and draws it rather towards the speaker or the artist (as though what he has to say were less important than the fact that it is he who is saying it—and less important than his virtuosity in saying it).

Where the work has the "nudity of spirit" of which she speaks, there should be no attention to what is likely to excite admiration. The spirit in the final judgement shall be nude, since adornment puts a screen between the person and the public. In this there is some connexion with the ring of Gyges, and with illusion. Also, and especially, the want of intellectual probity.

The quest for sensuality as the quest for pleasure. Evasion of suffering. So that one loses the sense of the pleasure as well. Love which would welcome pleasure and suffering equally. (As opposed to day-dream romances.)

Preoccupation with sensuality is meant to afford or provide gratification, but gratification of only one kind. Pain and suffering could afford gratification as well, but only when there is a sense of the worth or the importance of the beloved (or of the life of the beloved). This is what the "quest for sensuality" leaves out.

This may have something to do with the fact that this search for gratification commonly takes the form of an obsession—of something which distracts from other things which one may be doing, or to which one gives importance. In some way this is connected with vanity (I imagine this is especially clear in D. H. Lawrence). Wanting to bestow upon oneself the care or gratification which in other circumstances one might want to bestow upon the beloved. This may be one reason why it commonly gives an impression of childishness—obviously in Lawrence's case. A child who never gets beyond a consideration of what he is getting.

But when we say this, perhaps we make the issue look simple. It is not. And the chief trouble lies in what Plato called the beauty which there is even in the object of sensual desires. Perhaps this is not always so; but there may well be a certain beauty in writing or in music which does not have the severity which Simone Weil seeks, and which would be called "erotic." It is easier to say this in general terms than it is to say anything precise. Scriabin's "Poème d'Extase"[14] may have little or nothing one could call beautiful. (Liszt's Liebestraum or still more vulgar rubbish.) The difficulty is to say what happens when people do love such music: whether Plato would say that they do sense, in however confused a way, some reflexion of beauty.

If Simone Weil speaks as she does about Villon, what would she say about Goethe? Clearly he was not interested only in his own sensations; he had a deep sense of good and evil. (Distinguish between Werther and Faust.)[15]

NOTES

From Notes dated 7.8.62; 4.3.62; 29.7.63; 31.8.63; 7.9.63; 27.10.62; from a letter to M. O.'C. Drury dated 14 February 1963; and Notes dated 12.4.64; 19.7.64; 18.6.63.

1. "Toute amitié vraie passe par le Christ," *Intuitions Pré-Chrétiennes*, Paris: La Colombe, 1951, p. 140.

2. "Human Personality" in Richard Rees (ed. and trans.), *Selected Essays 1934–1943*, Oxford: Oxford University Press, 1963, pp. 9–34.

3. "Ne pas parler de Dieu (pas non plus dans le langage intérieur); ne pas prononcer ce mot, sauf quand on ne peut pas faire autrement (<<peut>> a ici évidemment un sens particulier)." *Cahiers* III, p. 143.

4. Simone Weil, "La Personne et le Sacré," in *Écrits de Londres et Dernières Lettres*, Paris: Gallimard, 1957, pp. 11–44.

"L'autre cri si souvent entendu: 'pourquoi l'autre a-t-il plus que moi?' est relatif au droit. (. . .) Pour former les esprits capables de résoudre les problèmes situés dans ce domaine, l'École de Droit suffit.

Mais le cri: 'pourqoi me fait-on du mal?' y pose des problèmes tout autres, auxquels est indispensable l'esprit de vérité, de justice et d'amour." Ibid., p. 38.

"Le mal infligé du dehors à un être humain sous forme de blessure exaspère le désir du bien. . . . Quand la blessure a pénétré profondément, le bien désiré est le bien parfaitement pur. La partie de l'âme qui demande: 'Pourquoi me fait-on du mal?' est la partie profonde qui . . . ," ibid., p. 39.

"De même la personne ne peut être protégée contre le collectif, et la démocratie assurée, que par une cristallisation dans le vie publique du bien supérieur, qui est impersonnel et sans relation avec aucune forme politique." Ibid., p. 43.

"Cet ordre impersonnel et divin de l'univers a pour image parmi nous la justice, la vérité, la beauté. Rien d'inférieur à ces choses n'est digne de servir d'inspiration aux hommes qui acceptent de mourir." Ibid., pp. 43–44.

"La vertu d'illumination et de traction vers le haut réside dans ces mots eux-mêmes, dans ces mots comme tels, non dans aucune conception. . . . Dieu et vérité sont de tels mots. Aussi justice, amour, bien." Ibid., p. 42.

"La beauté est sensible. . . . Elle n'a pas non plus de langage; elle ne parle pas; elle ne dit rien. Mais elle a une voix pur appeler. Elle appelle et montre la justice et la vérité qui sont sans voix." Ibid., pp. 37–38.

"Autant le malheur est hideux, autant l'expression vraie du malheur est souverainement belle. . . . L'éclat de la beauté est répandu sur le malheur par la lumière de l'esprit de justice et d'amour, qui seul permet à une pensée humaine de regarder et de reproduire le malheur tel qu'il est." Ibid., p. 37.

5. "Le temps à proprement parler n'existe pas (sinon le présent, comme limite), et pourtant c'est à cela que nous sommes soumis." *Cahiers* I, Paris: Librairie Plon, 1951, p. 114.

6. "Travailler—si l'on est épuisé—c'est devenir soumis au temps de la même manière que la matière. La pensée est contrainte de passer d'un instant au suivant. C'est là obéir." *Cahiers* I, p. 127.

7. "Celui qui doit travailler tous les jours sent dans son corps que le temps est inexorable." Ibid.

8. "Das Gefühl ist nämlich daß die Gegenwart in die Vergangenheit schwindet, ohne daß wir es hindern können. Und hier bedienen wir uns doch offenbar des Bildes eines Streifens, der sich unaufhörlich an uns vorbeibewegt und den wir nicht aufhalten können. Aber es ist natürlich ebenso klar, daß das Bild mißbraucht ist. Daß man nicht sagen kann, >die Zeit fließt<, wenn man mit >Zeit< die Möglichkeit der Veränderung meint." Ludwig Wittgenstein, *Philosophische Bemerkungen*, Frankfurt: Suhrkamp, 1981, §52, p. 83.

9. "Une vie entièrement libre serait celle où toutes les difficultés réelles se présenteraient comme des sortes de problèmes, où toutes les victories seraient comme des solutions mises en action." *Oppression et Liberté*, p. 116.

10. "On ne peut rien concevoir de plus grand pour l'homme qu'un sort qui le mette directement aux prises avec la nécessité nue, sans qu'il ait rien à attendre que de soi, et tel que sa vie soit une perpétuelle création de lui-même par lui-même." *Oppression et Liberté*, p. 117.

11. "Une ombre impénétrable enveloppera toujours le rapport immédiat qui lie nos pensées à nous mouvements." *Oppression et Liberté*, p. 120.

12. "Parfois les réactions du corps vivant sont complètement étrangères à la pensée." *Oppression et Liberté*, p. 120.

13. ". . . sans qu'il ait rien à attendre que de soi, et tel que sa vie soit une perpétuelle création de lui-même par lui-même." *Oppression et Liberté*, p. 117.

14. A. N. Scriabin, "Poem of Ecstasy" (4th Symphony).

15. J. W. von Goethe, *Die Leiden des Jungen Werther*, Frankfurt: Insel, 1989, pp. 1–149. Idem, *Faust*, Frankfurt: Insel, 1989, pp. 6–441.

CHAPTER TWELVE

GRACE AND THE
BEAUTY OF THE WORLD

"What does Simone Weil mean when she speaks almost as though atheism might be a form of religious belief? What then is the difference between an atheist and a believer? What difference would it make if there were no religion in the world? or nothing which were recognized as religion?"

It is not hard to see what she means when she speaks of atheism as a purification from idolatry, although perhaps you should be familiar with some of the examples she gives of 'idolatry'. But if we said this of atheism, it would be purely negative: from saying that it is a purification from idolatry, it does not follow that it is a practice of religion. And I do not think she meant to suggest that it would be.

She would have said that a man might be a declared atheist and yet "obey the commands of God"; and that there might be a love of God in his beliefs and practices, even though he did not recognize this. (Remember that belief in God and the love of God are the same for Simone Weil.) But this would mean that in *addition* to being an atheist he showed a love of the world, at least in the form of amor fati, and that he showed compassion for people in distress, whether from social oppression or, for instance, widespread famine—a compassion which was also humility, which was free from any thought of personal loss in such suffering (the loss one might feel when the suffering afflicted those to whom one was specially attached). This need not go with atheism, although it may, and often has. And although it is an addition to atheism, it need not include any explicit love of God, or any explicit recognition of God.

155

The notion of the 'love of the world' is difficult—for many people, anyway. Simone Weil seems to have thought commonly of the amor fati of the Stoics. But I am not sure whether this always has a reference to 'the world', as religious writers have understood this when they have spoken of "God and the world."

More important for her is the notion of 'the world' which she associates with science. For it is here that the notion of 'the beauty of the world' comes in. But I do not want to start along this road at the moment.

If we do leave "love of the world" in the background, then we might ask: granting that an atheist shows constant compassion and that he shows a selfless devotion in his desire to relieve distress, how does he differ from many humanists? Simone Weil did not think that humanism had much or anything religious about it. But then how could she say that there might be a real love of God in such an atheist?

One might almost ask (and I have heard something like this objection): "Then does it make any difference whether you bring in religion or whether you do not? Is all the talk about God, which comes into religion—is all this really superfluous or empty?"

"A world without God." This phrase is confusing. But for Simone Weil it might mean, for example, a world without Grace. All right. Suppose someone asks then: what were the difference between a world without Grace, and a world *with* Grace? (Or: "Can you *conceive* of the natural world without the supernatural? And if so, what would you add if you thought of the natural world together *with* the supernatural?")

For Simone Weil the commonest examples of what she calls "supernatural" are in the lives of men—in what we might call the presence of divine Grace in men. Perhaps most obviously in humility. I may desire to be humble, I may wish I could keep from considering *myself* in relation to everything I do and everyone I meet. But I cannot become humble—lose my regard for myself—by resolving to do so. I cannot get there by my own will, or by an exercise of my own efforts. For if I do, or if I try to, then I shall think of humility as an *achievement*. Almost as though I might count that gain in my advance towards humility. This were an example of what Simone Weil calls "mensonge" (lying, untruthfulness). My achievement would be a form of phariseeism or pride.

The most I can do is to desire that I might somehow, sometime, show genuine humility (probably without realizing that anything of the sort was happening). At the same time I may come to recognise more clearly the different forms (and the persistence) of complacency, self-satisfaction, contempt, envy, etc. There is value in this, but it is not in itself the achievement of humility.

I might then say that if ever I do act with humility, it will be a matter of luck. It will not be my own doing, nor will it come through my exercise of my own wisdom. It is something similar to this when Simone Weil says that if any man acts with humility, this is by the Grace of God.

Objection: "When Simone Weil speaks of Grace, there is the idea of God behind it. You speak of the matter in terms of 'luck'. Do you mean that it makes no difference whether you describe it in the one way or the other? Is she not referring to anything when she speaks of God? Is it just a matter of phraseology?"

If the words I used seem drained of religion—if they do not seem to bring God in at all—then the word 'humility' is not being understood as Simone Weil would have meant it. I speak of humility, not as a posture or an attitude of mind which one may adopt. Or could you speak of doing the same thing, sometimes with humility, sometimes without it? Could you speak of coming to someone's assistance in this way, as though the humility or the want of it were a difference in the way your act was clothed? (If my neighbour asks me to forward his post while he is away, and I say I will, I may do this willingly or I may do it unwillingly. Either way, I do forward his letters. And if I start doing it with some resentment, I may even argue myself out of this—tell myself not to be a fool—and change my attitude to what I am doing. But I wonder whether you could speak of 'with humility' and 'without humility' in this way. I do not think that you could.)

(By the way, why is false or "assumed" humility so particularly loathsome?)

"Without humility, no man can show compassion for another." This does not tell you *how* to show compassion for another. It tells you something of what we mean by 'compassion'. Or we might say: it tells you something of what compassion is.

And similarly: if Simone Weil says that it is only through the Grace of God that one can act humbly, she does not mean that the Grace of God is an external help by which the humility is brought about, as the fair weather may put me in a good temper, or as your words may help me to go on when I am tired and had begun to waver. For I do not think she would distinguish between the humility and the Grace of God.

"Something of what compassion is." For Simone Weil it is the contemplation of beauty. She comes back to this again and again. I have said that 'humility' and 'compassion' are not two separate ideas. The contemplation (or recognition) of beauty is not something different from humility either.

(Amour propre defiles the beauty of that which you see. Or comes between you and the beauty that is there; prevents attention and contemplation.)

"Concentration and attention is the attitude that corresponds to beauty. . . . Humility is the primary characteristic of attention."[1]

She thought of compassion as a humanist would not.

> Il y a dans la pauvreté une poésie dont il n'y a aucun autre équivalent. C'est la poésie qui émane de la chair misérable vue dans la vérité de sa misère. Le spectacle des fleurs cerisier, au printemps, n'irait pas droit au cœur comme il fait si leur fragilité n'était tellement sensible. En général une condition de l'extrême beauté est d'être presque absente, ou par la distance, ou par la faiblesse. (. . .) La condition humaine, c'est à dire la dépendance d'une pensée souveraine, capable de concevoir et d'aimer ce monde et l'autre, rendue esclave d'un morceau de chair qui lui-même est soumis à toutes les actions extérieures, cela est beau. Qu'il y ait la beauté, c'est infiniment mystérieux. Mais en fait il en est ainsi. (. . .) La richesse anéantit cette beauté, non pas en apportant un remède à la misère de la chair et de l'âme soumise à la chair, car aucun remède ne nous est accordé ici-bas, mais en la dissimulant par un mensonge. C'est le mensonge enfermé dans la richesse qui tue la poésie. C'est pourqoi les riches ont besoin d'avoir le luxe comme ersatz. (. . .) Un petit bistro, où sont dévorés pour quelques sous de repas sommaires, est plein de poésie à en déborder. Car il est vraiment un refuge contre la faim, le froid, l'épuisement; il est placé sur la limite, comme un poste frontière. Cette poésie est déjà tout à fait absente d'un restaurant moyen, où rien ne rappelle la possibilité que des hommes aient faim.[2]

"But just as one consents to one's own affliction when it comes upon one, so one must consent to that of others, when it is *absolutely* impossible to prevent it, but with the same irreducible bitterness" (*Notebooks* Vol. I, p. 258).[3]

"To love God through and beyond the destruction of Troy and of Carthage—and without consolation. Love is not consolation, it is light" (*Notebooks*, Vol. I, p. 258).[4]

If we spoke of humility as 'luck', we should add that it is a light or illumination. In the form of compassion, it is what makes it possible to look on (or contemplate) human affliction—from which all one's "natural" instincts turn away. An illumination of human affliction—without reducing the dreadfulness or the horror of it. If we speak of compassion as love, it is the love which holds us in the contemplation of beauty, and in this sense it is not personal.

This would be an "implicit" form of the love of God. But it might come to someone who never spoke of it as the love of God, and who never spoke (even to himself) of the presence of God.

The *spiritualité du travail*, as Simone Weil thought of it, would be related to the same sense of the "poésie de la condition humaine." I will not try to discuss this here. But it illustrates what she is saying constantly: that although God be "absent," the contemplation of God in ordinary life would not appear in turning away from the world; it would appear in the way in which one was able to look on the world. (I say in "ordinary life" because I will not try to discuss the mystical experiences.)

"A way of looking on the world." These words by themselves could mean almost anything, or nothing.

Spinoza spoke of viewing things, or viewing the world, *sub specie aeternitatis*. I do not think this covers much of what Simone Weil meant when she spoke of the beauty of the order of the world, for instance. No doubt she would have agreed with certain of his criticisms of the notion of 'final causes' and of 'providence'. And when he is speaking of the 'amor intellectualis dei' he makes some remarks which she might have echoed: when Spinoza says, for instance, that this love of a human mind for God is part of the infinite love by which God loves himself—although I do not think she ever took this just as he did. "The love of this beauty proceeds from God dwelling in our souls and goes out to God present in the universe" (Simone Weil, *Waiting on God*, p. 120).[5] I do not think she would have spoken of this love of beauty as *amor intellectualis*—not even when she is speaking of the beauty of the world which is discovered through science. I do not know what Spinoza meant by 'amor' in that phrase. But I cannot find in him anything like her conception of beauté: the beauté in which she could contemplate human affliction and evil. "L'univers est beau . . . le sentons." ("The beauty of the universe . . . we sense it.") In comparison with remarks like this, Spinoza's observations seem superficial: his conceptions of good and evil, especially, but also his conception of la condition humaine subject to circumstances, to oppression and to affliction.

It is the same point if we say that he had only the most superficial discussion of what it is to be "subject to time." He speaks of "illusion" or "imagination," and of "inadequate knowledge," which are found when a man's life is not "a life of reason." But I cannot find in him anything akin to the sense in which Simone Weil speaks of illusion or of mensonge. And for this reason the question of salvation, or freedom from such illusion, this question could never arise for him in the sense in which it does for her.

For Spinoza, the life of "servitude" to the passions is a life in which one is forever selling one's birthright for a mess of potage. "He who increaseth knowledge increaseth sorrow," since with such knowledge I may see more clearly what sort of life would be worth living (what sort of life would not be futile or empty), and yet this knowledge is helpless against those passions which prevent me from living such a life. The sorrow of a life at the mercy of circumstance. If a man could gain freedom from this servitude (and Spinoza thought he could show how this might be), then he might also attain to that "peace of mind" which recognizes how things are and perhaps finds joy in this. In other words, for Spinoza the "love of God" should *liberate* one from sorrow, and should show how to live so as to avoid it. (This should come from an *understanding* of the world, primarily an understanding of the laws of mechanics.)

Simone Weil did not think that the beauty of the world can be *understood*, in the sense in which we speak of understanding in science. We cannot try to understand the affliction and the evil of la condition humaine; but we cannot try to understand the beauty of it either. (Almost as though we might explain *why* this is beautiful. In the face of disasters it is common to ask, "Why do such things happen?" We do not so often ask, "Why is that beautiful?" But it would be the same sort of question.)

Spinoza had no conception of salvation as Weil thought of it. For he had no conception of affliction or of love. "Love is something divine. If it enters the human heart, it breaks it. The human heart has been created in order to be broken in this way. The saddest waste occurs when it is broken by something else. Even so, it prefers to be broken by anything at all, other than divine love. For divine love only breaks those hearts that consent to it being so. Such consent is difficult."[6] This is not a search for "peace of mind." And if it were. . . . How much compassion enters the life of Spinoza's "free man"? The "peace of mind" Spinoza sought would not be *Grace*. It would be something a man might achieve through his own efforts. Comparison, as Simone Weil thought of it, is not the desire to "do something about it," or to get *rid* of evil. If it were . . . then it would not be a recognition of beauty, and it would not be the love of God. (Recognition of beauty: recognition of God humiliated and crucified.) This is where she is furthest from the humanists.

You may look on a landscape and be vaguely aware of its beauty, or perhaps even indifferent to it. Or you might be powerfully struck by the distress and suffering you have come upon, and you may feel so strongly, "We must *do* something about," that you think of nothing else. And in doing something about it, you may behave towards the afflicted person with 'superbia': organizing, doing good, putting things right. Humiliating the sufferer where you should have humbled yourself.

The humanist emphasis may be on human happiness—"improving, raising the lot of man." Making a better world. Solidarity—"we've all got to stick together" (which is likely to be tyrannical).

Contrast: "What is your torment?" (Quel est ton tourment?)

The difference between Simone Weil and pantheism depends on her notion of *time*. So do her notions of 'obedience' and 'love of God'. She holds that in order to appreciate beauty seen, you must have some sense of it as transitory. "It is a condition of great beauty that it be nearly absent, at a distance, or fragile."[7] The *fragility* and perishability of human existence is essential to its beauty. The *distance* of beauty.

Because Spinoza did not see the relation between life—suffering—time, he did not see the relation between eternity and death. Love is eternal—"purify your hearts, ye double minded"—in Plato and in Simone Weil. What meaning would this have in Spinoza?

Humanism: as though the lot of man could be measured by freedom from, or lessening of human distress. Compare the conception of 'faith in man'. In this way it comes between me and my recognition of the beauty of the world; or my recognition of divine love. "When it enters the human heart, it breaks it" (cf. p. 7, note 24).[8] This is what is entirely lacking in Spinoza.

pacem relinquo vobis, pacem meam do vobis . . . (peace I leave unto you, my peace I give to you).

By letting himself be nailed to a cross between two thieves and spat upon—so that his closest followers could see nothing of God there and went away, pacem relinquo vobis.

Opening their eyes.

Simone Weil: conception de l'enfer: fausse béatitude, se croire par erreur au paradis. Deliverance de l'enfer. (Conception of hell: false beatitudes, erroneously thinking oneself in paradise. Deliverance from hell.)

pacem. The third movement of Bruckner's Eighth Symphony.

Choosing the capital punishment of a slave. Where God's love appears—in what was done as a matter of routine to those who were regarded as hardly a subject of pity. Et incarnatus est. Ecce homo. non quomodo mundus dat, ego do vobis.[9]

"No man cometh unto the Father but by me" (*Notebooks* I, p. 282).[10]

Beauté. Musique—imitation du silence. Purité. (The distinction between beauté and "sham" beauty: what is taken for it because it has a strong appeal in other ways.) It is only through contemplation of beauté that we can have a conception of divine love. (We are not left merely with "analogy" to human love.) This is the point of calling music 'imitation of silence', where the sense of divine love is also the sense of the eternal: music as showing the relation (or the contrast?) of the eternal and time (or process). The sense in which music, and especially the beauty (or greatness) of music, is impersonal.

Her constant use of the term 'beauté' is confusing; I wish she had considered aesthetics more precisely: the difference between 'beauty' and 'greatness', or what Kant called "das Erhabene" (the sublime). Whether one would speak of the "beauty" of a storm. Or whether one would call *King Lear* "beautiful."

For Simone Weil, "the beauty of the world," "the soul of the world" ("Incarnation") is connected with understanding the world. And this latter, for Simone Weil, seems to be understanding the universal law or universal harmony; seeing the ways or forms in which this (??) harmony is evident; seeing how apparent disharmony could be explained, and so on. Beauty as the manifestation (or existence?) of eternity—what is eternal—in time.

To someone for whom the word 'God' has no meaning, 'Incarnation' can have none.

I can understand something of the ways in which people (some, many) use the word 'God'; I can see that it is natural to look up when one says "God help me." And I can understand something (not clearly) of the sort of help one may cry for when one cries to God. Similarly (though again not very clearly) with praising God; hymns and religious rites. The sense of wonder at birth, at death, and so forth.

How is such a sense of wonder joined with "moral aspiration," with the conception of a life which is worthless or worth living? (Could there be any such aspiration without a sense of evil and of sin?)

The ideas of 'the world' and of 'reality': there are difficulties in thinking of *evil* as "error," as perhaps in some sense an *illusion* or illusory. What were meant by saying either that the world—or reality—is evil (pessimism: it were better not to be, but also it were better if there had been nothing) or that the world/reality is good? If any and every existence is good, then the existence of something evil is good, and so on.

The eternal in time: naïf objections.

If God *became* a man, then for that time God *was* a man—with human weaknesses (at least physical weaknesses: he was not self-sufficient).

To say that God was born at a particular time implies that what occurred before this time occurred in the absence of God. "Before Abraham was, I am." Does anyone understand this use of 'I'? If God is a man living in a *particular* place, then God is not universal: related to everything in the same way, and so on. If you say that "*as man*, he is not God," then you give up the case: there is no incarnation of God. (God is "absent" and "in heaven.") St. Paul seems to say both that "he emptied himself of his divinity" and also that as man he was divine and still God.

There are difficulties with the idea of 'a perfect man'. (A man without blemish, without a stain, immaculate.) Compare 'perfect justice' or 'perfectly just': "I can find no fault in him." The idea of *what justice requires*. Whether anyone ever "fulfills these requirements to the full," so that there were no ground for criticism: you could not imagine any respect in which it could have been done better. (St. Paul and the Epistle to the Romans.) I find this strangely academic and unreal. Related somehow to Phariseeism. Compare rules for the right way of fulfilling prescribed offices, perhaps in a monastery.

I may be dissatisfied with what I have done; and I may wonder whether it was right after all. But I do not know what would be *meant* by asking whether the action was *perfectly* right. You may say: "Don't ever think that there is no room for improvement." But this does not give me the idea of someone in whom there *is* no room for improvement.

The question: "What is important about my life?" Wittgenstein's suggestion that someone is happy, or has found the answer to the problem of life, who is prepared to die at any time. But still seeking for reward, or compensation, or whatever will give sense to the life that is profoundly unsatisfactory.

If death is thought of as solemn and sombre, this has not been so much because it is a misfortune to him who meets it, as that it is rather a thought which makes one think of everything else in life differently: it has no place among projects; it is nothing which can be an object of investigation.

Why is it that one sets such importance on that which one is striving after or trying to get (success etc.)?

Simone Weil says that it is "an illusion that there is some positive value in my own existence." Compare the idea that 'with death I shall lose everything'. Suppose a miser said this of his treasure.

I always hope I may come to understand her remarks better. But this would take character (what she would call purity, perhaps) as well as intelligence, which I do not have; and what I "understand" is mostly dim guessing.

I do not think all her remarks (about death, for instance) would be quite compatible with one another, though it is easy to be stupefied about this. And if they are not, I do not think this matters: it is what you would expect.

"Death is the most precious thing that has been given to man. That is why the supreme impiety is to make an improper use of it. Dying amiss. Killing amiss. (But how escape at the same time both from suicide and murder?) After death, love. (Similar problem: neither an improper gratification, nor an improper deprivation.) War and ἔρως (eros) are the twin sources of illusion and falsehood among men; their mixture constitutes the greatest form of impurity" (*Notebooks*, Vol. I, p. 103).[11]

"Life and death of others. To be happy that there are thinking beings other than oneself; essential form of grace. To desire the death of a human being is to reject this form of grace (cf. Creon).—But to be happy, also, to be mortal, that they are mortal; both for oneself and for them, to the same degree. Never to desire one's own death, but to accept it" (*Notebooks*, Vol. I, p. 57).[12]

I will quote one remark from *La Connaissance Surnaturelle*, which may be related to these in certain ways:

"God suffered in place of man—this does not mean that the affliction of Christ has reduced, by however little, the affliction of men, but that through the affliction of Christ (equally in the centuries before and in the centuries after) the affliction of everyone afflicted takes on a significance and the value of an expiation, if only he desires it. The affliction then takes on an infinite value which can come only from God."[13]

Suppose it be said that in death we come nearer to God. That we stand face to face with things, without dreams or illusions. I think I understand something of this.

And (though my statement makes it sound commonplace) it is important to be able to view one's life in relation to death. Momenti mori.

But this does not mean that death—or something that happens in death—is the only thing that is really important. (Or that whatever is unsatisfactory in life will be seen to be significant in relation to death.)

Simone Weil sometimes seems to say that the existence of any human (or other) creature has no positive value, or even that it is an evil (an affront against God?). But she was not able to hold this, for instance, when she was concerned with lives other than her own, as she generally was. Or even in much of what she says of beauty—of the beauty of a mortal and fragile existence, like that of cherry blossoms, for instance.

It would be a disastrous mistake to *forget* death, and, *nota bene*, in connexion with any object of natural beauty (cherry blossoms) or any saintly life. But there is something important in that *life*: important that it is mortal, certainly, and we should not know what importance we are talking about otherwise. But it is important that there have been, and maybe are, human beings whose lives are like that. That is important for our attitude towards human beings and human life generally. That there are (or have been) human beings for whom it would be worth making any sacrifice, for instance.

NOTES

From Notes dated 4.9.64; from a letter to M. O.'C. Drury dated 5 May 1968; from undated Notes.

1. "Le regarde et l'attente, c'est l'attitude qui correspond au beau . . . L'humilité est avant tout une qualité de l'attention."

2. Simone Weil, "Fragments et Notes," in *Écrits de Londres*, Paris: Gallimard, 1957, pp. 180–81. "There is a poetry in poverty which has no equivalent elsewhere. This poetry emanates from the poverty-stricken flesh, seen in the truth of its poverty. The spectacle of cherry-blossoms in spring would not go straight to the heart as it does if their fragility was not so perceptible. It is, in general, a condition of absolute beauty to be almost absent, at a distance, or fragile. (. . .) The human condition, that is to say the dependence on an intellect which is not only sovereign enough to understand and

love this world and the next, but also enslaved to a piece of flesh that is itself subject to all sorts of external happenings—this is beautiful. How there can be beauty in this, is totally mysterious. But it is, in fact, so. (. . .) Wealth destroys this beauty, not by remedying the destitution of the flesh and the soul that is subjugated to it, as no remedy is granted us down here, but by concealing it with a lie. It is the lie locked up in affluence that murders the poetry. That is why the rich have need of luxury as *ersatz*. (. . .) A little bistro, where basic meals are had for a few pence, almost overflows with poetry. For it is a veritable refuge from hunger, cold, exhaustion; it is situated on the threshold, like a border post. Such poetry is already entirely absent from the average restaurant, where nothing reminds of the possibility that men might be hungry."

3. "Mais comme on consent à son propre malheur quand il survient, aussi à celui d'autrui quand il est *absolument* impossible de l'empêcher, mais avec le même amertume irréductible." *Cahiers* II, p. 180.

4. "Aimer Dieu à travers la destruction de Troie et de Carthage, et sans consolation. L'amour n'est pas consolation, il est lumière." *Cahiers* II, p. 181.

5. "Amour de cette beauté procède de Dieu descendu dans notre âme et va vers Dieu présent dans l'univers." Simone Weil, *Attente de Dieu*, p. 123.

6. "L'amour est chose divine. S'il entre dans un coeur humain, il le brise. Le coeur humain a été créé pour être ainsi brisé. C'est la plus triste des gaspillages quand il est brisé par autre chose. Mais il préfère être brisé par n'importe quoi plutôt que par l'amour divin. Car l'amour divin ne brise que les coeurs qui consentent à l'être. Ce consente est difficuile."

7. "Une condition de l'extrême beauté est d'être presque absente, ou par la distance, ou par la faiblesse." "Fragments et Notes," in *Écrits de Londres*, Paris: Gallimard, 1957, p. 180.

8. "S'il entre dans un coeur humain, il le brise."

9. And he became incarnate. Behold the man. Not as the world gives, give I unto you.

10. "Nul ne va au Père sinon par moi." *Cahiers* II, p. 218.

11. "La mort est ce qui a été donné de plus précieux à l'homme. C'est pourqoi l'impiété suprême est d'en mal user. Mal mourir. Mal tuer. (Mais comment échapper à la fois au suicide et au meurtre?) Après le mort, l'amour. (Probléme analogue: ni mauvaise jouissance, ni mauvaise privation.) La guerre et ἔρως (eros) sont les deux sources d'illusion et de mensonge parmi la hommes; (leur mélange est la plus grande impureté)." *Cahiers* I, p. 163.

12. "Vie et mort des autres. Être heureux qu'il y ait des êtres pensants autres que soi; grâce essentielle. Désirer la mort d'un être humain, c'est refuser cette grâce (cf. Créon).—Mais être heureux, aussi, d'être mortel, qu'ils soient

mortels; pour soi-même et pour eux, au même degré. Ne jamais désirer sa propre mort, mais l'accepter." *Cahiers* I, p. 93.

13. "Dieu a souffert au lieu de l'homme—cela ne signifie pas que le malheur du Christ ait diminué . . . le malheur des hommes. . . . Le malheur prend alors une valeur infine qui ne peut venir que de Dieu." *Connaissance*, p. 104.

CHAPTER THIRTEEN

EVIL, DEATH, AND SUFFERING

ACCEPTANCE

The folly of imagining ways of "getting *rid* of evil," "a state in which there is only justice," "a life of absolute purity," and so on.

Étienne Borne on the dilettante (refusal to commit oneself), the miser, and the pharisee: different techniques for keeping evil at a distance; the social or political fanatic who knows the cause of all evil in society or history and would root it out.[1] Sorel connects such fanaticism with optimism. The importance of pessimism, at least: of realizing that there can be no question of getting rid of evil or of destroying it. The opposite is the way from pessimism to cynicism, which is, once more, ingratitude and a refusal to recognize dependence. (Cf., also, those to whom God has spoken, "forests of the night.")[2] The evil one who knows all the answers. Fanaticism: "the war to end wars." The revolution: the complete and final conflict. ". . . they are evil because, right from the start, they have refused to submit their evil acts to the anguish that is the sole path to liberation." (*Is* there a voie vers la liberation? Is there not some ground to suspect any claim to 'la *seule* voie'?)[3]

"But the *acceptance* of evil amounts to indifference." Kant's idea of moral perfection ("from duty alone"). A morality which is not *contaminated* by "anything empirical." The view that all desires are evil. Simone Weil "Elle n'étant jamais . . . pour soi." A terror of impurity. Desire to be out of reach of impunity by one's own conscientiousness. (A Catholic might say: refusal to leave it to God—refusal to recognize that one's salvation depends on this. Simone Weil's idea of a *mechanism* of

Grace puts on the human being a responsibility for perceiving it.) The dangers in "You have no duty to do what is beyond your powers." But also in the opposite—in denying it (Grete Hermann and Nelson).[4]

"If you say I must *not* strive after perfection—leave this to God, perhaps—does not this lead to complacency and contentment with what I am?" How to distinguish: "*accepting* what you are" and "being content with what you are"? If I say "I know I shall never be really (or wholly) free of hypocrisy," this does not mean that I do not think it is very important to avoid it. Or consider: being discouraged by my failure to avoid what I know it is important to avoid. "If it is going to be like that, then life *is* just evil—as my life is." (In this situation any question of wanting to, or being willing to, "renounce the world" [because of *its* evil?] is just irrelevant.)

The sense of 'le misère humaine'. Is Simone Weil clear on whether the sense of one's own viciousness is included in this? If it were, then this would be one form of human misery—and the most serious—which Christ did not know. And his humility must have been different. She emphasizes that he knew the terror of being abandoned both by men and God (cf. her account of evil as "violation"). But what did 'abandoned by God' mean here? Abandoned to *evil*? Surely not. In one sense perhaps we can say that he experienced greater suffering than any human being. But we cannot say he experienced the depths of *human* suffering. Suffering injustice, suffering evil. ("Pourquoi fait on moi du mal?") (Why am I being harmed?) Being driven towards suicide by one's own moral failures. I imagine Kierkegaard paid more attention to this latter than Simone Weil did. Simone Weil's emphasis is on suffering or subjection to *material* forces: iron, gravity, and so on. (Does this stem from her earlier Marxist ideas?)

"Take up thy cross. . . ." Be resigned to the person that you are. Conferre Kierkegaard. "Vernünftelt nicht . . ." (Do not rationalize . . .).[5] Simone Weil: "I do not want to change the world in any way at all. I do not want to interfere with the realm of necessity: that is to say, with decreation. I want to submit myself."

SACRIFICE

The dreariness of most of religion at the present day. In so far as the Catholic Church escapes this at all, it is through the concentration on the Mass. Most of the preaching and most of the Catholic writings are dreary enough. And I wish the churches could be places of worship simply, rather than places for denunciation and uplift.

In saying this I am really talking of what I do not know, since I believe the most important work of the Catholic Church is often in the confessional; and I have no experience of this. I know that it is believed to do what some of the Protestant churches have relegated to sermons. I need not add that the value depends on the confessor, and that some priests have a special talent for this, while others—probably the greater number—have little. The confessional at any rate has the merit, as I understand it, of trying to meet problems which the people themselves bring. I imagine that the problems are more often moral than religious, but I know nothing definite about this.

I have wished that the church might concentrate on helping its devotees to a better understanding of matters in worship, and of moral questions which are connected with these, rather than on trying to extend its influence, or on trying to induce half-hearted churchgoers to show greater devotion, and so on. I cannot imagine that this kind of exhortation instils much devotion; for I think devotion is nourished from coming into contact with it, but that it springs from difficulties and from reflexion.

There is a remark of Simone Weil's about a statement by Father Perrin that he had now baptised eighteen adults. She says that this emphasis upon numbers makes the whole thing like the attitude of a miser towards his gold. Diverting attention from the supernatural. (Where thy treasure is there will thy heart be also.)

Some who have come near to the Church and are deeply grateful for what they have found there have been disturbed by certain encouragements to become a Catholic and be one of us. For there is something in this which reminds one of encouragements to join a political party. And some of the things which are said about "the work of the Church" have the same overtones. Catholics commonly hold back, and do not press, but they speak about the growth of the Church in a way that disturbs nevertheless.

Does it matter so much whether the whole world be converted to Christianity? Is not the Church, by *trying* to achieve this, losing its own spirit?

I do not think I am suggesting that there should be just Carthusian orders and nothing else. Probably that were impossible anyway. But there are many of us who cannot give our lives to prayer like that—who cannot even understand it—who would still welcome what could be done to deepen our devotion: the devotion of those whose lives are in temporal affairs.

Von Hügel's emphasis upon joy is common among Catholic writers and preachers now. It may be partly—in this part of the world, anyway—in order to counter the gloom of Calvinism. To counter any emphasis on the Ten Commandments which stays negative as they are, and which does not supplement them with the command to love. For I imagine that joy and love must be pretty much the same. I think love would be what Simone Weil had emphasized anyway. The love of God and the love which goes with any apprehension of the beauty of the world.

Theologians have criticized this emphasis on beauty, finding in it an attempt to deny the reality of evil. But I do not think this can apply to Simone Weil. Certainly it implied in one sense an acceptance of evil; or such a recognition of it as is itself compassion. The kind of recognition of it which we find in the Book of Job and in the Greek tragedies and in *King Lear*, for instance. She remarks that whereas the contemplation of evil is generally unbearable, the portrayal of it by great artists may be supremely beautiful. And in this we see how the recognition of the evil of the world may still be a love of the world and a sense of the beauty of the world.

It goes together, too, with her joining of love and justice. I imagine that without this she might hardly have dared speak of God's love. Anyway, with regard to other people she emphasizes both justice and compassion. And she is able to keep these distinct from friendship. (See the essay, "Forms of the Implicit Love of God" in *Waiting on God*.) I like especially the remarks which are given in *Gravity and Grace*. Friendship is not what is commanded in the command to love thy neighbour. "It is one of those things which are added unto us" (*Gravity and Grace*, p. 59).[6] And compassion, which requires deep humility, requires also that one keeps one's distance. "What are you going through?"

"Religion is joy" is too short to serve by itself. It has been said too often and too seriously that religion is suffering, where this does not mean either that religion is breast-beating nor that it is the endurance of sin and hardship alone. Both the joy and the suffering of religion have been understood in very different ways. And it seems easy to fall into an (apparently) insincere vulgarisation of them. Simone Weil wrote more about affliction and about suffering than she wrote about joy. There were many reasons for this, but I imagine one of them was a feeling that the misunderstandings of suffering and affliction were deeper and more difficult to sort out. Again and again she comes back to the danger of missing the significance of affliction in one's relation to God: the danger of turning Christianity into a worldly religion, as she says that Judaism was. I am thinking, for instance, of something she says about martyrdom, and the difference between martyrdom and Christ's crucifixion: "At the contact of the iron one must think oneself separated from God as Christ was, otherwise it is a different God. The martyrs did not feel that they were separated from God, but then it was another God, and perhaps it would be better not to be a martyr. The God in whom the martyrs found joy in their tortures and in their death was near to the one officially adopted by the Roman Empire and imposed in the exterminations which followed" (perhaps not included in *Gravity and Grace*). (I suppose she means the adoption by Constantine; the most obvious of the exterminations would be that of the Albigenses.)

This seems to be one of her deepest remarks. In one sense I feel sure she profoundly admired the martyrs, and of course their martyrdom was not something which they themselves sought. And yet . . . the suffering of Christ was something different, that is, *becoming man* was something different. And if you do not see this, you do not understand the relation of the creature to God. Neither do you understand the teaching of Christ's life and what Christianity requires of one: "God could not come to earth, become flesh, and remain perfectly pure, except by undergoing the most extreme suffering" (i.e., including the suffering of feeling abandoned by God).

She has another remark about the crucifixion which I like, part of which is included in *Gravity and Grace*, although the translator's English almost kills it (e.g., for 'offering' read 'sacrifice'; otherwise you lose all the force): "The mystery of the Cross of Christ lies in a contradiction, for it is both a willing sacrifice, and at the same time a punishment to which he is subjected in spite of himself. If you looked only on the sacrifice, you might even will this for yourself as well. But you cannot will to be subjected to punishment against your will."

"Those who think of the crucifixion only in terms of sacrifice erase the mystery and the bitterness through which it brings salvation. To desire martyrdom is to desire far too little. The cross is infinitely more than martyrdom."[7]

And—I suppose to explain the expression 'the mystery and the bitterness which brings salvation'—she adds: "The *irreducible* character of the suffering"—meaning, I suppose, the suffering which cannot be brought lower—"which makes it impossible to keep from horror as soon as one is subjected to it, is designed to arrest the will, as absurdity arrests the intelligence, and as the absence or non-existence arrest love. Until, when he has reached the limit of human faculties, a man reaches out his arms, stops, looks and waits.

The looking and the waiting—this is the attitude towards beauty. As long as you can still think, will, desire, beauty will not appear."

I had wanted to say something of her remarks about death, for these interest me especially. But I have wandered pointlessly for too long, and I must leave that for another time. She puts death and love together as two great blessings to men. And she will not agree that a belief in eternity implies a denial of death. Or that the reality of eternity diminishes the reality of death. There is the remark about belief in immortality in *Gravity and Grace* (p. 33), but in the *Notebooks* this is preceded by the remark, "One must entirely accept death as annihilation."[8] And this comes at the end of some very interesting discussions of the importance of death for the belief in God. (By the way, the translation in *Gravity and Grace*, p. 33, ends ". . . and it robs death of its purpose." I do not think 'purpose' is right. The French is 'et ôte l'usage de la mort'. I would rather say, "and robs death of its importance."[9])

For one thing, she recognizes something of what Wittgenstein called "the majesty of death," when he was speaking of the rites of primitive peoples. The sense of this seems to me to have gone out of our lives, for the most part. Death is something which happens in hospitals (and in the newspapers). It is an unfortunate accident, to be passed over as quickly as may be. I think this helps to make our view of life shallow, and it helps to kill all sense of our relation to the world of living things. Just as we have little sense of our relation to our grandparents and ancestors. But the chief importance lies in the kind of thing Simone Weil is saying, and this is religious.

I should like especially to consider what she says of the relations of death and love. This is connected with her view of the love of God, and of the sacrifice of self which goes with this. But there is more in the ideas as well, I think.

COMPASSION

The influence of medicine on our view of human lives and human difficulties, on our view of human life, and on our thoughts about human affairs appears in the common view of human suffering at the present day. People think of human suffering as some sort of mistake, or something which the advance of medicine has not yet managed to deal with; but given time we shall be able to put it right. With the progress of medicine (and of genetics and other sciences) suffering can practically be stamped out. Compare Ernest Jones's remark that "sheer unhappiness has become a medical problem." Suffering is a blemish which is there because we have not yet succeeded in growing human life as it should be grown. It does not in any sense belong to what we *mean* by human life. If we could really produce human life as we think of it in science—and as we mean it in science—then it would be *without* suffering.

> Not all our songs, my friend, can make death clear,
> Or make life bearable.

The medical view keeps us even from *asking* whether life is bearable. We are not able to think of *understanding* life, in the sense in which great composers and dramatists and poets have tried to understand life. Life does not present any problem which it is difficult to understand. We can think only of understanding how to *improve* human life ('la dolce vita'), and we can understand this better and better with the growth of medical and other research.

And just as we are not able to ask about life, so neither can we see any significance or importance in death. Death is just the end of a process. Or it may be an unfortunate accident, like the smashing of a vase.

This takes all the meaning out of compassion. It takes all the *depth* out of compassion, just because it takes all the significance and all the mystery (or problem) out of suffering. We are left with 'compassion' in the sense of: "What a pity, especially when it might have been prevented."

On this view, then: if there is suffering, this shows only that human beings are ignorant or that they have mismanaged. When we have added to our knowledge and perfected our methods . . .

This is part of the general idea that the lives we have or the lives we lead depend on human contrivance and management. (We 'have' them because our lives are supplied to us, or are part of the productive enterprise of organizing human society and arranging human destiny.) In this case, 'What is the meaning of it all?' would be a question without sense. Equally—or still more—the question, "What is the meaning or significance or the importance of the *end* of life?" We can no more ask, "What is ended?" than we can ask "What has been going on?" The blowing of a trumpet which calls the living man or sounds the end—this would have no meaning whatever.

Compassion. "She is a woman who, if she hears of something terrible, at once thinks that she ought to try to do something about it." The idea seems to be: "If you did *not* feel that you must do something about it, then you would be showing indifference. Or insensitivity." This is curious, and I think it is plainly mistaken. But it has influenced ideas of compassion; and generally it has degraded it.

There is more love of other persons, and more appreciation of suffering, if you look on suffering with an amor fati. What Simone Weil says about 'le vide' is connected with this, and with her view that it is a confusion to think that 'good' is what meets or satisfies human needs— even if we include needs which must be met if it is to keep alive. This is one reason why it is misleading if you start to speak of religion as something which answers to a need in men. If you turn your attention to needs in this way, then you deceive yourself or make yourself blind. (You erect a screen to shut out your view.)

She did not think there was any merit in mortification of the flesh. Or that asceticism had any value on its own account. Thibon seems to have misunderstood her here. She thought it important *not* to go in search of what will meet your bodily needs and desires. This went with the view she took of her own suffering, and the view she thought anyone should take of his suffering. It went with her view that you take a false view of suffering if you think first and foremost that you ought to do something about it.

"Keep from thinking that you can compensate for the suffering— that you can balance or neutralize it—if you can obtain this or that which you desire. Or that you can cure it by taking these or those measures."

Weil did not see any value in *creating* suffering. But she did see idolatry in becoming devoted to any earthly means of appeasing the suffering. The importance of maintaining a state of unsatisfied desire is just the importance of maintaining purity in the love of God, or maintaining purity in her thought of God. "The love of God is not a consolation, it is a light."

Compare with this the way in which some people discuss sexual desires, and the importance of developing "a personality" or "an ego" which will be able to meet and cope with the difficulties in one's relations with other people.

This view speaks of withdrawal from relations with other people—the wish to preserve one's solitude—as though it were obviously defective.

The first comment might be that such a life may well be defective in achieving the kind of life which these psychologists seem to admire. (Sexual fulfilment and other sorts of fulfilment.) But equally plainly, the balanced life which meets the "reality" of relations with other people, which has an integrated personality and so on, would be defective in and blind towards the sort of purity and devotion which Simone Weil thought important. I have said already that this psychological view is superficial in its view of suffering. Vide Freud, for instance.

These psychologists see a very limited range of problems, within a narrow frame of conceptions, regarding uncertainty of one's own identity, being afraid of the people you meet, and so on. They are all made to appear as forms of childishness. And it looks as though the psychologists could not understand problems of any other sort. All problems seem to be rooted in arrested development of some sort or other. And if only there could be full development, then all would be well. They write as though there were never much difficulty in understanding what full development is.

VOCATION

A Catholic woman said to me that she would not try to live in poverty in the way Simone Weil did, and that she knew she would not be able to do so, adding, "I know I have no vocation for it." She said nevertheless that she thought it was a wonderful thing that someone like Simone Weil *was* able to live in this way; that it did show a wonderful (and I think she would have said "inspiring") example of what can be done, inspiring even to those who have no vocation for it themselves.

This notion of 'I have no vocation for it' is not always easy for someone who is not a Catholic to understand. If you consider it superficially, it seems a convenient way of excusing yourself from any very difficult or very unusual obligation. But this is not how it was said in the case I am mentioning.

It is an important corrective to a certain kind of "perfectionism" preached by some Kantians. Compare Grete Hermann's discussion of Nelson's ethics. On the other hand (but I do not know that this contrasts with the position of Grete Hermann), consider the parable of Jesus: ". . . I have married a wife, and therefore I cannot come," and so on.

The notion of a vocation for the priesthood, for example, is fairly clear. There are many men of whom one would say that they ought never try to become priests, no matter how sincere, determined, or resolute they were. And similarly, of course, with a woman entering a convent.

Something of this idea has probably been taken over into the "professions" like medicine, law, teaching, and so on. Or rather, there *was* something of this idea at one time. And here it becomes allied with the notion of *talent*, although this has little or no analogy with religious vocation; neither would it have made sense if the Catholic woman had said that she had not the *talent* to live a life of poverty in the way Simone Weil did. If she had said that, then the reply "That is no excuse" would have been relevant and sensible.

"Und muß es das *Klavier* sein?" (Does it have to be the piano?)

"And must it be *philosophy*?" It is natural enough to speak of a talent for philosophy, or a want of it. On the other hand, people have also spoken of a vocation here; Simone Weil in particular would have done so, I think. (Cf. the beginning of her *Cahiers de Londres*.)

"Trying to help other people." "Having no vocation for helping other people." It is probably important to distinguish between different kinds of "help" (I am not thinking merely of the relativism which John Anderson used to emphasise).[10] There are certain sorts of help which I ought never to try to give, no matter how strongly I might wish to do so.

"'Doing good'. Whatever I do, I know perfectly clearly that what I am doing is not 'good'. For what I do cannot possibly be good, from the mere fact that it is I who do it. Only he does good who is good; he who is not good cannot do good. And 'God alone is good'.

We must not say: 'It is good that I should do so and so'; but 'It would be bad if I didn't do it'" (*Notebooks*, Vol. II, p. 417).[11]

This is because "the essence of the necessary differs from that of the good" (*Notebooks*, Vol. II, p. 434).[12]

> It is as though a man who is keeper of a huge and powerful beast had got to know its tempers and its desires, how best to approach and how best to handle it, when it has its sulkiest and when its mildest moods and what causes them, on what occasions it is in the habit of uttering its various cries, and what sounds will soothe or provoke it. Now, suppose him, after he had got to know all these things from long experience of the animal, to call this knowledge wisdom, and systematizing it into an art to take to teaching. He has

no true knowledge as to which of these beliefs and desires is beautiful or ugly, good or bad, just or unjust. He employs all these terms in accordance with the opinions of the mighty beast, calling things that please it good, things that displease it bad. Other reason for his use of these terms he has none, but calls what is compulsory just and good. He has never perceived, nor could he teach another, the vast difference which really exists between the nature of the compulsory and the good. (Plato, *Republic*, 493)

Consequently, "I have not the principle of sinning in me" (*Notebooks*, Vol. II, p. 434).[13]

There are certain sorts of evil which I ought not to try to remove (no more than I ought to try to prevent the dying of love between two people). I shall only make things worse.

Wittgenstein: "You cannot lead people to the good; you can only lead them somewhere. The good lies outside the space of facts." (B. F. McGuinness [ed.], *Wittgenstein and the Vienna Circle*, Conversations recorded by Friedrich Waismann, Oxford: Blackwell, 1979, 117n 82).[14]

The evil (or sometimes it is merely confusion) of feeling that one is called on to put the world to rights.

Ad absurdum: "I shall fail in my duty unless I become a saint and unless I rid the world of evil."

The frequent confusion between "I have failed in my duty" and "what I have done includes much that is evil"; "I have nothing on which to congratulate myself"; "I am still as bad as I was (pray God I am not worse)"; and so on. The Kantian seems to me often to make this confusion. And it seems to me to come in part from Kant's confused idea that my overriding duty is to do my duty. With this may go the sort of confusion which Grete Hermann discusses in particular, that the most important duties—in this sense perhaps the fundamental duties—are the same for every man. See especially articles p. 77 and 78. Examples of vocations, p. 77 infra. (Grete Henry-Hermann, "Conquering Chance," trans. Peter Winch, in *Philosophical Investigations* 14, 1991, pp. 48–49).[15]

Against this the Catholic notion of vocation is important. This notion itself becomes dangerous when it leads into ideas of hierarchy ("those who have higher vocations have also greater responsibilities," and this notion of "higher vocations" may easily come to be seen as "deserving of higher respect") and of authority.

I feel like saying: "It becomes dangerous when it is associated with Aristotelianism."

"A priest is more holy than a bus conductor."

"A priest is a *better* man than a bus conductor."

"A priest is more deserving of respect than a bus conductor—what he says should be listened to; what he does should be given approval"—even what he says and what he does *outside* those special activities which require the vocation for the priesthood.

Gaining—learning—a deeper moral insight. When you learn about morality, and especially come to appreciate distinctions which you had not noticed heretofore—much of this is what might be called "conceptual clarification." Changing your way of looking at moral questions.

"Moral perplexity" is not *simply* trying to understand your own ideas. "Ich kenne mich nicht aus." (I do not know my way about.)

But one of the deepest forms of moral perplexity is at any rate not something which springs from our ignorance of vital information. Granting you have all the information—all the "facts"—which is relevant, you may still find it impossible to decide.

This is one respect in which the preoccupation with such moral problems is like the preoccupation with the problems of philosophy.

On the other hand, familiarity with philosophical discussions, and, if you like, with philosophical "techniques," may not make you any better able to come to a decision on a moral problem of this sort.

("Can it give some assurance that the decision you *do* finally reach will be the right one?")

Schubert: *Die Schöne Müllerin*

The beauty (charity, compassion) in the portrayal of a terrible situation in which a human being goes to pieces: in which life is "impossible."

Seeing *in* this situation the beauty, the love of God. It is of this that Schubert was capable. And this capacity appeared in the compassion (and *detachment*) with which he himself viewed (contemplated) it. His talent or his greatness in music cannot be separated from this. Nor vice versa.

Viewing one's own sufferings and afflictions—misfortunes—in this way. The saints have done this, I suppose.

But viewing the evil one does, not only my own blunders and failures through my fault, but the terrible things I have done, how can this stand? How to see the love of God in this? Or see this as any sort of beauty, without falsifying it?

If at all, then it must be connected in some way with the ability—or decision—to keep going in spite of what I have done.

The religious sense of "hope"? Misericorde divina (divine mercy).

When Simone Weil is writing about *malheur* (there is no English equivalent, but the translators use 'affliction' to give something not just equivalent to 'suffering') she says, for instance, that evil is neither suffering nor sin, "it is both of these at once, something common to the one and the other; for they are linked, sin brings suffering and suffering degrades or makes a person vicious, and it is this indissoluble mixture of suffering and sin that is the evil in which we are in spite of ourselves." She speaks of the possibility of "dissociating" the vice and the suffering which are "indissolubly" mixed in this way. If this happens, it does not reduce the suffering, but it is possible then that the suffering shall not be an object of horror, as it is in the degrading and degraded 'mixture'. ("Suffering ceases to be mingled with viciousness; and on the other hand the viciousness is transformed into simple suffering.") She speaks of this as "a supernatural operation which we call repentance." I do not understand this, although I have no doubt that she knows what she is talking about. I think I do understand a little of what she means when she speaks of affliction as a mixture—or an intermingling—of suffering and sin or viciousness (e.g., envy, the kind of dejection which Spinoza called pride, and so forth). And I can understand, at least vaguely, her remark that in certain conditions, which one cannot simply produce at will, it is possible to dissociate the suffering and the viciousness.

She is blessedly far from the hollow suggestion of some persons that "suffering ennobles one." Prolonged physical pain can degrade and destroy the soul. But then it has become also something besides physical pain. For one thing, it has already seized hold on the soul and shackled its attention. Just because of this, no exhortation to the person so afflicted will help. He is likely to resent it, to be bitter against the person who is so little affected that he is able to make such an exhortation, and so on. Pure or genuine charity, coming from understanding rather than from "desire to help," could start a change; at least I think Simone Weil would say this. But a man cannot show charity, no more than he can show humility, by resolving to do so. If he tries that, he will take satisfaction in his achievement, which, therefore, will be phariseeism, not charity. So, where I would say that if anyone does act with humility or in charity, this is luck, not his own doing, she would say it was supernatural grace.

When I say, "charity could start a change," I mean: if the afflicted person *meets* with charity from someone. My language might suggest that I was thinking of his showing charity in his affliction. But this is impossible, at least until he meets charity from another, in which case he *may* show gratitude, which is akin to it; and Simone Weil would say this goes with repentance, I think. This is how I understand her writing, but it is likely that I have it wrong.

NOTES

From undated Notes; a letter to M. O.'C. Drury dated 9 April 1962; Notes dated 21.1.63; 31.1.63; 29.12.64; 31.12.64; a letter to Vernon Yeates dated 15 May 1969.

1. Étienne Borne, *Le Problème Du Mal*, Paris: Presses Universitaires De France, 1960, p. 112.

2. "forests of the night," cf. Blake, "The Tyger."

3. ". . . ils sont le mal parce que dès le départ ils ont refusé cette participation au mal dans l'angoisse qui est la seule voie vers l'libération," Borne, *Problème Du Mal*, p. 112.

4. See Grete Henry-Hermann, "Conquering Chance," trans. Peter Winch, *Philosophical Investigations*, Vol. 14, No. 1, January 1991. This essay appeared first in *Leonard Nelson zum Gedächtnis*, ed. Minna Specht and Willi Eichler, Frankfurt a. M.—Göttingen, Verlag Öffentliches Leben 1953: "Die Überwindung des Zufalls."
See Leonard Nelson, *System of Ethics*, trans. Norbert Guterman, New Haven: Yale University Press, 1956. The volume Grete Henry-Hermann discusses. *Critique of Practical Reason* is the first volume of Nelson's *Lectures on the Foundations of Ethics* and is available in libraries in translation on microcards. (Ed.)

5. I. Kant, "Groundwork of the Metaphysic of Morals," trans. H. J. Paton, New York: Harper and Row, 1964, pp. 57–58, 65f.

6. "Elle est de ces choses qui sont données par surcroît," Simone Weil, *La Pesanteur et La Grace*, Paris: Plon, 1948, p. 77.

7. The published version reads: "Those who can only conceive of the crucifixion under the aspect of an offering do away with the salutary mystery and salutary bitterness of it. To wish for martyrdom is far too little. The cross is infinitely more than martyrdom." *Gravity and Grace*, p. 89.
"Ceux qui ne conçoivent la crucifixion que sous l'aspect de l'offrande en effacent le mystère salutaire et l'amertume salutaire. Souhaiter le martyre est

beaucoup trop peu. La croix est infiniment plus que le martyre," Simone Weil, *Pesanteur et Grâce*, p. 103.

8. *Notebooks*, vol. II, p. 492.

9. The published version reads: "Belief in immortality is harmful because it is not in our power to conceive of the soul as really incorporeal. So this belief is in fact a belief in the prolongation of life, and it robs death of its purpose." *Gravity and Grace*, p. 33.

"La croyance à l'immortalité est nuisable parce qu'il n'est pas en notre pouvoir de nous représenter l'âme comme vraiment incorporelle. Ainsi cette croyance est en fait croyance au prolongement de la vie, et elle ôte l'usage de la mort." Simone Weil, *Pesanteur*, p. 43.

10. See John Anderson, "Realism versus Relativism in Ethics," and other papers on ethics in *Studies in Empirical Philosophy*, Sydney: Angus and Robertson, 1962.

11. "'Faire le bien'. Quoi que je fasse, je sais d'une manière parfaitement claire que ce n'est pas le bien. Car ce que je fais ne peut pas être bien, dès lors que je le fais. Car celui qui fait le bien est bon; celui qui n'est pas bon ne fait pas le bien. Et 'Dieu seul est bon'. Non pas: 'il est bien que je fasse cela'; mais 'il serait mal que je ne le fasse pas'." *Cahiers*, III, p. 8.

12. ". . . de combien différent l'essence du nécessaire et celle du bien." Ibid., p. 33. Ref. to Plato's *Republic*, VI, 493c.

13. "Je n'ai pas en moi de principe d'ascension." *Cahiers* III, p. 35.

14. "Man kann die Menschen nicht zum Guten führen. Man kann sie nur irgendwohin führen. Das Gute liegt außerhalb des Tatsachenraumes." B. F. McGuinness (ed.), *Ludwig Wittgenstein und der Wiener Kreis*, Frankfurt: Suhrkamp, 1984, 117n 63c.

15. Grete Henry-Hermann, "Die Überwindung des Zufalls," in Minna Specht and Willi Eichler (eds.), *Leonard Nelson zum Gedächtnis*, Frankfurt: Verlag 'Öffentliches Leben', 1953, pp. 77–78.

CHAPTER FOURTEEN

NOTES ON THE
OLD AND NEW TESTAMENTS

"The Old Testament seen as the body without its head; the New Testament: the head; the Epistles of the Apostles: the crown on the head.

When I think of the Jewish Bible, the Old Testament on its own, I feel like saying: the head is (still) missing from this body. These problems have not been solved. These hopes have not been fulfilled. But I do not necessarily have to think of a head as having a *crown*" (Wittgenstein, *Culture and Value*, 1939–1940, p. 35e).

In the last remark there is something akin to Simone Weil's criticism of the Church. There is something similar in the following remark by Wittgenstein:

> The spring which flows gently and limpidly in the Gospels seems to have *froth* on it in Paul's Epistles. Or that is how it seems *to me*. Perhaps it is just my own impurity which reads turbidness into it: for why shouldn't this impurity be able to pollute what is limpid? But to me it's as though I saw human passion here, something like pride or anger, which is not in tune with the humility of the *Gospels*. It's as though he *is* insisting here on his own person, *and doing so moreover as a religious gesture*, something which is foreign to the Gospel. I want to ask—and may this be no blasphemy—: "What might Christ have said to Paul?"But a fair rejoinder to that would be: What business is that of yours? Attend to making *yourself* more honourable! In your present state you are quite incapable of understanding what may be the truth here.

In the Gospels—as it seems to me—everything is *less preten-
tious*, humbler, simpler. There you find huts; in Paul a church.
There all men are equal and God himself is a man; in Paul there is
already something like a hierarchy; honours and official positions.—That, as it were, is what my NOSE tells me. (*Culture and
Value*, 1937, p. 30e)

Simone Weil would have agreed that there are "prefigurations" of
the Gospels to be found in some of the Psalms, in the Book of Job, in
Isaiah, and in "the Wisdom books." "As for Israel, certain parts of the
Old Testament, the Psalms, the Book of Job, Isaiah, and the Book of
Wisdom, contain an *uncomparable expression of the* beauty of the
world."[1] But was it in this sense that the Evangelists spoke of particular
(and often apparently trivial) events and actions in the life of Jesus as
fulfilling the scriptures or fulfilling the prophecies?

She found in Job and the Psalms and Isaiah an apprehension or revelation of those truths which are timeless, although they are brought to
men at different times (and this is the descent of God), the same truths
which are shown more perfectly in the Gospels. In the passage I have
cited she is speaking especially of a sense of "the beauty of the world."
You will remember also that in her comments on the Lord's Prayer she
says that in the line 'sanctificetur nomen tuum' (hallowed be thy name'),
nomen (the name) is the Word of God, which cannot be pronounced by
human lips. "Man has access to this name, even though it is transcen-
dent. It shines in the beauty and order of the world and it shines in the
interior light of the human soul. This name is holiness itself, and there
is no holiness outside it. . . ." I suppose her point would be that in the
way he speaks of the beauties of nature, Isaiah makes us aware of the
work of God; perhaps even more by the way in which he speaks of suffering and of the Servant. And similarly with the Book of Job. When the
Gospels show the holiness of Jesus's life and Passion, they show the
word of God more perfectly.

But if the Gospel truth is prefigured in what psalmists and prophets
of Israel said, this is not saying that what Jesus did in this place or in
that fulfilled an ancient prophecy. (It was remarked long ago that many
of these prophecies would fit the life of Cyrus as well as they fit that of
Jesus.) Or must we understand 'prophecy' in a very different fashion? Is
this what St. Paul thought? I find it strange when he seems to read the
Old Testament as an allegory, teaching what Jesus taught (or what the

early Church taught). Perhaps this way of thinking of historical accounts was fostered by the apocalyptic writers, such as the author of the Book of Daniel (in which Schweitzer thought Jesus was saturated). And I suppose the early Church, with its idea of the imminent Second Coming, was often near to "apocalyptic ways of thinking." But I do not remember any saying of Jesus's in the Gospels which suggests that he read the O.T. books in this way himself.

If you do read the Old Testament as an allegorical account of what is said more plainly in the New Testament, then you do not think of it as a record of important *past* events. And you may wonder how you should take the *New* Testament. Is this an allegory too? or an historical record?

Did St. Paul mean that the Hebrew scriptures are an incomplete or hidden pronouncement of those arkana which cannot be spoken, but which he was shown when he was carried up into the seventh Heaven on the occasion of his conversion?

Consider the prophecies which the acts of Jesus fulfilled, including, for instance, the passages in Isaiah which have been taken to foretell his death and resurrection. Are not these *temporal* prophecies? predictions of temporal events? Were they not meant as the disciples on the road to Emmaeus took them when they hoped for a temporal redemption of Israel? And what was it that Jesus explained to these disciples? By expounding the scriptures to them, he showed that all this *had* to happen. This means, I suppose, that it was the will of God, and that this was what God's prophets had spoken to them. But . . . this seems to me to allow different interpretations, and I still do not understand. How, or in what sense, did the early scriptures make it easier to *understand* the Passion of Jesus? or how did they illuminate it?

Was Jesus showing to those disciples that his life and Passion *were* a redemption of Israel? and that their way of understanding the prophecies and the promise of redemption had been mistaken?

If so, why do the Evangelists often fasten on such curious events as evidence that the life of Jesus was what the prophets had foretold? I have not been able to understand the Evangelists in this. On the one hand they seem to suggest that orthodox Jews had misunderstood the promise of the Messiah—that they had not understood what it was that God had promised. On the other hand, they speak of "fulfilments of the prophecies" in the sense in which orthodox Jews would have spoken. And they do not make it clear (to me) in what sense those earlier statements of the prophets *were* prophecies of this which they had seen when they were with Jesus.

Of course I agree that the sayings of Jesus are full of allusions to Old Testament writings, so that often we should hardly know what he was saying if the Old Testament were closed. In some important way he thought of his mission in terms of the Old Testament teaching. It is said that he thought of himself as the Messiah of which the Old Testament writings speak. And some, who have studied the O.T. more carefully than I, have told me that the conception of the Messiah can be seen to be consistent throughout the Old Testament. I have been told that the phrase 'the Son of Man' belongs especially to the Book of Daniel; but about all this I have no opinion. I will agree—because I respect those who have told me—that I cannot understand what Jesus thought himself to be, unless I have understood what the Old Testament books meant by the Messiah. But here I have to plead want of understanding.

In any case, this can hardly mean that one could get a fairly full understanding of that message which Jesus brought, just by studying the Old Testament, and even if one had not heard of Jesus. For I suppose this would mean that the word of God was incarnate in certain earlier men and works, in something of the same sense as it was incarnate in Jesus.

I do not know that Simone Weil would have objected to saying this, but orthodox Christians would.

I have dallied so long in preliminaries that there is no time left for the question which you asked and which I wanted to consider. Simone Weil's criticisms of the religion of Israel are severe; and some people might think that in this field she is voicing an obsession or a prejudice. I would not say this myself, although I imagine that if she had lived longer she might have forced herself to see more of what was good in Israel. Jesus interpreted the supreme commandments differently from Moses (and he could be more bitter in his criticisms of the Scribes and the Pharisees than Simone Weil was towards the Jewish faith), but he does seem to have thought that in some sense the word of God was to be found there; and I imagine that this might have made her try to find more favourable readings of some of them. But I think the main part of her criticism would have remained. In what she did write—in the three or four years in which she wrote on religious questions—she suggested that the "source" of Christianity was in Greece. This is most emphatic in her *Letter to a Priest*,—which is not her best book.

I suppose her view of *time* was Greek and not Hebrew (others have said this). For the Hebrews time began with the creation of the world, and time would "go on" to the end of the world and then stop. The Greeks did not think of time as a movement from a beginning to an end, but they thought of time as circular just as they thought of all movement, or "the movement of things" as 'circular'. (This latter term might have various interpretations. It might include something like a pendulum: disturbance of "equilibrium" in one direction and possibly continuing imbalance in this direction until a certain limit is reached, then restoration of equilibrium, followed perhaps by imbalance towards the opposite extreme which again finds a limit and is followed by return to equilibrium, and so on.) The Greeks seem to have no view of "history" such as ours, which we have acquired from the Hebrews through Christianity. They were not inclined to think either of the totally antiquated or of the totally new. And they were less inclined to think of some one event as unique, or as that for the sake of which all the past had been. What is divine is "ageless and deathless": if it has shown itself now, it has shown itself before and will show itself again.

The Greeks were philosophers because they wanted to understand what they saw and what they thought and the lives of men as they knew them. They were not interested in achieving a greater future which should outshine all that there ever had been in the past. They did not feel impelled to join the race towards some future goal. This made them, I think, more open to compassion than the Hebrews were (though goodness knows the Greeks could be merciless enough on occasion). And it made them able to look for clarity rather than for novelty in their thinking.

The Greek strain is pretty strong in St. Augustine's thinking, I imagine; although other elements have been added as well. "Late, late have I loved Thee, Beauty most ancient, Beauty most new, too late have I loved Thee . . ."[2]

Simone Weil's view of time was fundamental to much else in her view of Christianity and of Israel. She could not think of a chosen people, for whom alone a Messiah should appear. And she sought for "intimations of Christianity" not only in the Greek poets and philosophers, but also in the folklore of other peoples (of *all* peoples, if she could have found and studied all).

NOTES

From a letter to M. O.'C. Drury dated 18 February 1964.

1. *Waiting on God*, p. 116.
2. Augustine, *Confessions* X, 27.1.

SIMONE WEIL

BIOGRAPHICAL AND
BIBLIOGRAPHICAL SKETCH

1909   Born in Paris on February 3, the second child of the physician Dr. Bernard Weil (1872–1955) and his wife, Selma (1879–1965).

1915   First attempts at writing poetry.

1916   Receives private tuition in Chartres.

1917   Student at the *Lycée Laval*.

1919   Enters *Lycée Fénelon*, a public school and junior college for girls in Paris.

1921   Starts to suffer from chronic headaches.

1924   Study of Philosophy at the *Lycée Victor Duruy*, where she passes the first part of her Baccalaureat exams, in Latin and Greek. Undecided whether to study mathematics or philosophy, she eventually opts for the latter.

1925   Second part of Baccalaureat passed in philosophy. Greatly influenced by Alain (1868–1952) at Lycee Henri IV. Study in Rome.

1928   *École Normale Supérieure*. Comes into contact with a revolutionary movement and develops an interest in Marxist thought and the condition of the working classes.

1929   First publications in Alain's "Libres Propos."

1930   Completes her diploma-monograph, *Science and Perception in Descartes*.

1931   Articles in "Libres Propos," "L'Effort," "La Révolution Prolétarienne." Teacher of Philosophy at the girl's lycée of Le Puy.

---

*Based on Angelica Krogmann, *Simone Weil* (Rowohlt: Hamburg, 1991), 169–176.

1932   General strike in Le Puy and protest marches, in which she takes part. Compulsorily transferred to a girl's school in Auxerre.

1933   Teaching position at girl's lycée in Roanne. Interests in political sociology begin to form. Demonstrations in St. Etienne, and protest marches of the mineworkers, whom Weil addresses in a speech, carrying the red flag of solidarity. Leo Trotsky and his wife visit the Weil family.

1934   *Réflexions sur les causes de la liberté et de l'oppression sociale.* Manual labour at electronics firm Alsthom. Experiences recorded in *Journal d'usine* and *Expérience de la vie d'usine.*

1935   Repeated unemployment. Lycée in Bourges. Takes an interest in Gregorian music and regularly attends early morning prayer in Bourges Cathedral.

1936   Associate editor of the newly founded "Nouveaux Cahiers." Outbreak of Spanish Civil War. She joins the Republicans in Barcelona, but an accident forces her to return to France.

1937   Teacher at the lycée of St. Quentin. *La condition ouvrière.*

1938   Experiences a mystical revelation during a retreat at the Benedictine Abbey of Solesmes. Her writings begin to reveal a strong interest in religion and the supernatural.

1939   Hitler occupies Prague. Weil abandons her pacifism in order to fight against the Hitler régime. *L'Iliade ou le poème de la force.*

1940   Association with *Les Cahiers du Sud* and *Les Cahiers d'Études Cathares.* Reads the *Bhagavad Ghita* and studies Sanskrit. Illegal activities in the résistance, for which she distributes leaflets—"Cahiers de Témoignage Chrétien"—in the unoccupied French zone. Arrested for "Gaullism," interrogated and put under surveillance by the Vichy police. Further deepening of her social and religious concerns.

1941   Encounter with the nearly blind Father Jean-Marie Perrin at the Dominican monastery in Marseilles. Perrin becomes her spiritual mentor. Studies in Greek philosophy, Hinduism, and Sanskrit. *Pensées sans ordres sur l'amour de Dieu.*

1942   Studies of Plato and Pythagorean philosophy, as well as of pre-Christian revelations (later published as *La Source Greque* and *Intuitions Pré-Chrétiennes*). Letters to Father Perrin, later published in *Attente de Dieu.* The fourth letter contains her spiritual autobiography. Leaves with Perrin's friend Thibon about a dozen notebooks with daily reflections, a compilation of which is published in 1947/8 under the title *Le Pesanteur et la Grace.* The notes are published in their entirety in 1951 as *Cahiers* (Notebooks).

1943 Moves to Britain and takes a room in London. Here, she works for Forces de la France Libre (F.F.L.), and goes on hunger strikes in support of starving countrymen in German-occupied France. Writes *L'Enracinement*. Enters Middlesex Hospital, but refuses medical treatment and food. Receives visits of a Catholic priest, but refuses to be baptised. Later in the autumn, she is admitted to Grosvenor Sanatorium in Ashford/Kent, where she continues to take no food. Dies on August 24 of starvation and pulmonary tuberculosis. Her *Nachlaß* contains diaries written in New York and London, with entries continuing until her move to Ashford, published in *La Connaissance surnaturelle*. From 1947, Weil's works are published in quick succession by Plon and Gallimard, Paris.

SIMONE WEIL

PUBLICATIONS

Attente de Dieu (Paris: La Colombe, Editions du Vieux Colombier, 1948).
English: *Waiting on God* (London: Routledge & Kegan Paul, 1951).

Cahiers I–III (Paris: Librairie Plon, 1951/1953/1956).
English:*The Notebooks of Simone Weil* (London: Routledge, 1956).

La condition ouvrière (Paris: Gallimard, 1951).

La connaissance surnaturelle (Paris: Gallimard, 1950).

Écrits historiques et politiques (Paris: Gallimard, 1960).
English: *Selected Essays 1934–45* (Oxford: OUP, 1962); selections only.

Écrits de Londres et dernières lettres (Paris: Gallimard, 1957).
English: selections also published in previous entry.

L'Enracinement (Paris: Gallimard: 1949).
English: *The Need for Roots* (London: Routledge, 1952), foreword by T. S. Eliot.

Essais, lettres et fragments, vol. 1 (Paris: Gallimard, 1965).

Intuitions Pré-Chrétiennes (Paris: La Colombe, 1951).
English: *Intimations of Christianity* (London: Routledge, 1957), also contains
    material from *La source greque* (see below).

Lettre à un religieux (Paris: Gallimard, 1951).
English: *Letter to a Priest* (London: Routledge, 1953).

Oppression et liberté (Paris: Gallimard, 1955).
English: *Oppression and Liberty* (London: Routledge, 1958).

La pesanteur et la grace (Paris: Plon, 1947).
English: *Gravity and Grace* (London: Routledge, 1952).

Pensées sans ordre concernant l'amour de Dieu (Paris: Gallimard, 1962).

La source grecque (Paris: Gallimard, 1955).
English: selection in *Intimations of Christianity* (see above).

Sur la science (Paris: Gallimard, 1966).
English: *On Science, Necessity, and the Love of God* (Oxford: OUP, 1968), selections from *Sur la science*; *Source grecque*, and *Pensées sans ordre*.

Index